Community

Community

A Contemporary Analysis of Policies, Programs, and Practices

Katharine Kelly & Tullio Caputo

UNIVERSITY OF TORONTO PRESS

Library and Archives Canada Cataloguing in Publication

Kelly, K. (Katharine)

Community : a contemporary analysis of policies, programs, and practices / Katharine Kelly & Tullio Caputo.

Includes bibliographical references and index.
Also issued in electronic formats.
ISBN 978-1-4426-0366-0

1. Community-based social services—Canada. 2. Community-based social services—Canada—Case studies. I. Caputo, Tullio, 1950– II. Title.

HV105.K44 2011   361.971   C2011-906174-0

We welcome comments and suggestions regarding any aspect of our publications—please feel free to contact us at news@utphighereducation.com or visit our Internet site at www.utppublishing.com.

North America
5201 Dufferin Street
North York, Ontario, Canada, M3H 5T8

2250 Military Road
Tonawanda, New York, USA, 14150

ORDERS PHONE: 1–800–565–9523
ORDERS FAX: 1–800–221–9985
ORDERS E-MAIL: utpbooks@utpress.utoronto.ca

UK, Ireland, and continental Europe
NBN International
Estover Road, Plymouth, PL6 7PY, UK
ORDERS PHONE: 44 (0) 1752 202301
ORDERS FAX: 44 (0) 1752 202333
ORDERS E-MAIL: enquiries@nbninternational.com

The University of Toronto Press acknowledges the financial support for its publishing activities of the Government of Canada through the Canada Book Fund.

Typesetting: Em Dash Design

Printed in Canada.

For Peter
and
For Mary Anne

This project would not have been
possible without your support,
patience, and understanding.

Contents

Acknowledgements

This book would not have been possible without the support of many people. We wish to express our sincere gratitude to the multiple communities and community members across the country who shared their thoughts and insights with us. Without their willingness to participate in our numerous studies, this book would not have been possible. We also want to thank Wanda Jamieson and Liz Hart who worked with us on a number of the projects on community activity. Our partnership with them has been a wonderful source of knowledge and intellectual growth. We also extend our thanks to those groups and agencies who funded or supported our studies: Carleton University, the National Crime Prevention Centre, the Youth Services Bureau, the Federation of Canadian Municipalities, and the RCMP. Our special thanks to Mary Anne Caputo for all her tireless work copy editing, checking references, and assisting us in bringing the whole project together. Special thanks also to our wonderful editor Betsy Struthers for meticulous work on the manuscript and her thoughtful comments and insights. Finally, we would like to acknowledge Anne Brackenbury and the team at the University of Toronto Press. In particular, thanks to our reviewers who provided us with invaluable insights and guidance.

Chapter 1

BRINGING COMMUNITY BACK IN?

Introduction

COMMUNITY—some celebrate its vibrancy, some mourn its loss, some seek to recreate it, while others argue it has never existed. Community is an elusive yet frequently invoked concept in Canada and throughout the world. Terms like community health, community living, community schools, community policing, community development, and community renewal have become part of the contemporary lexicon; they refer to what are often taken-for-granted features of the social landscape. Indeed, as Creed points out, we are seeing an "obsession—one with global reach that occupies politicians, activists, scholars, and laymen [sic] alike—the obsession with community" (2006, 1).

Why? What has led to the current interest and attention being paid to community by groups and organizations, particularly by Western governments, and why has it occurred at this point in our history? Why has it become the focus of issues ranging from crime, to poverty, child welfare, and even mental health—issues that not long ago were the sole domain of state agencies (Bellefeuille and Hemingway 2005)? What has caused the increasing acceptance that the community should be the primary vehicle through which a wide variety of government programs and services are delivered? And what has this shift of government focus onto the community meant for those living and working in communities?

These and related questions are explored in this book. To fully understand what has been occurring requires consideration of the political economy of the shift to the community by state agencies, a shift in which the community has become a central feature of the social and policy rhetoric of most contemporary Western democracies. Our analysis reveals that as a result of a political shift to NEOLIBERALISM, the state in Canada and other Western nations has increasingly sought to cut the costs of social support programs and has achieved this, in part, by DOWNLOADING responsibility for the delivery of programs and services to

1

the community level. This process is one example of the broader set of changes ushered in by neoliberal governments around the world, and it has led to a dramatic restructuring in the role of the state and the way government services and programs are organized and delivered. In turn, these changes have had a profound impact on communities and their members, including those working in a wide range of community agencies and organizations.

BOX 1.1: NEOLIBERALISM

Neoliberalism is both a philosophy and political approach to governing that emerged in a variety of forms in most Western democracies during the late 1970s. It is:

> a loosely demarcated set of political beliefs which most prominently and prototypically include the conviction that the only legitimate purpose of the state is to safeguard individual, especially commercial, liberty, as well as strong private property rights (cf. especially Mises 1962; Nozick 1974; Hayek 1979). This conviction usually issues, in turn, in a belief that the state ought to be minimal or at least drastically reduced in strength and size, and that any transgression by the state beyond its sole legitimate purpose is unacceptable (ibid.). These beliefs could apply to the international level as well, where a system of free markets and free trade ought to be implemented as well; the only acceptable reason for regulating international trade is to safeguard the same kind of commercial liberty and the same kinds of strong property rights which ought to be realised on a national level (Norberg 2001; Friedman 2006). (Thorsen and Lie n.d.)

We need to be clear. Governments have historically recognized and included the community in social policies. However, the nature of this inclusion has taken a dramatic turn over the past 20 to 30 years. Some have described this as the RESPONSIBILIZATION of the community, a process that involves shifting responsibility for social support primarily from the central government onto local communities—the people, groups, and agencies working at the local level (George 2008; Larner 2006; Mahon 2005; Rose 1996, 1999). This marks a significant shift away from a welfare state approach in which state agencies play the primary role in providing social support services.

An important implication of this shift has been that in downloading responsibility to the community, the state requires an identifiable community with which to work. That is, communities must become "known entities." They must be identified and their features mapped and classified in order for the state to decide with whom it can and cannot be involved. Once this is done, interventions must be planned, implemented, and assessed. Those communities and their members selected by the state must accept increasing responsibility for meeting local needs and responding to local demands—a role that was played by the state itself in the recent past.

As a result of these developments, communities are being made responsible for taking prudent measures to reduce crime, improve health, and mobilize needed resources on behalf of their members. They are exhorted to identify at-risk, in need, or dangerous elements of the population living within their midst and are made responsible for finding the means for responding to the challenges these populations pose. These changes have resulted in important alterations to the social and political landscape of this country and other Western nations that have followed a similar neoliberal path.

The impact of the move toward the community by the state can be seen in recent policy shifts that have altered the way services and programs are designed and delivered as well as in the practices followed by agencies working in communities. From this perspective, the move toward the community reflects what policy-makers describe as a return to community-based solutions and local action. This contrasts with an earlier approach in which citizens' needs were met through social programs established and run by centralized state authorities. That is, prior to the emergence of neoliberalism, social programs such as family allowance, unemployment insurance, publicly funded health care, education, workmen's compensation, and institutional care for those with mental health issues were provided by the state as part of the SOCIAL SAFETY NET. These programs and their provision were the hallmark of the welfare state approach. With the introduction of neoliberal polices, programs, and practices, the basic elements of the social safety net have been reduced or eliminated in favour of relying on market forces and making individual citizens more responsible for their own well-being.

Importantly, the adoption and development of a neoliberal approach has not meant that the state has given up control over what happens ON THE GROUND. In fact, while federal, provincial, and territorial governments have downloaded responsibility for social services and programs to community-based groups and organizations, they have sought to retain control over the agenda. They have done this in part through their control over the funding process. More recently, they have introduced various strategies such as requiring those providing programs and services to be more accountable for the way they spend public funds. They have also required those receiving funding to engage in more extensive evaluations of their work. However, while community groups and organizations have been forced to adapt to the changing policy and funding environment, as explored in the following chapters, they have not simply acquiesced to state demands but have responded in a variety of interesting and sometimes provocative ways.

This chapter considers a brief history of research on community; definitions of the concept and their implications on the ground; the use of community in policy development; and the implications for bringing the community back in, in terms of the ability of communities to meet and respond to the challenges of recent policy shifts. Chapter 2 provides an overview of the emergence of neoliberalism in the last decades of the twentieth century, including a discussion of the implications of this development for the move toward the community by the state. This is followed by a more in-depth examination in Chapter 3 of the question of who can legitimately claim to be a member of any particular community and the various ways that this can influence what actually happens for those living and working there. Chapter 4 analyzes the strategies developed by the state for the exercise of power resulting from the move toward the community. Chapter 5 considers the impact of government policies on practice, specifically their influence on how agencies working in communities have responded. The book concludes with a discussion of the implications of the move toward the community for social policy and practice as well as for the lived experiences of those living and working in communities.

Community in Social Research

The concept of community has a long and rich history in Western scholarship. It has played an important role in social theory and philosophy as people have tried to grapple with the changes they observed in the society around them. In fact, concern over community has been an important element of social thinking from the time of the ancient Greeks, including Plato and Aristotle (Bruhn 2004). It came to the fore, however, at the beginning of the nineteenth century when the rise of industrialization, immigration, and increased urbanization dramatically altered the social landscape. In particular the rapid growth of cities challenged the basic relationships that had characterized the largely rural and agricultural societies of the previous feudal era in which most people lived their entire lives in small towns or villages surrounded by family and friends and depended on those around them for support and assistance.

With the rise of industrialization and the growth of cities, more and more people left rural areas. As a result, they lived less and less in close-knit kinship groups. The norm in the burgeoning cities was for people to live in nuclear families consisting of two parents and their offspring. At the same time, people began to work at increasingly diverse and specialized jobs that further separated them from each other. During this transformation, communal life was slowly replaced by the increasingly individualized and atomized life of urban dwellers. These changing social relationships had a significant impact on the nature of society, including many undesirable consequences. For example, commentators from Charles Dickens to Karl Marx decried the growth of slums, grinding poverty, high unemployment, inadequate housing, and lack of proper sanitation, as well as the prevalence of disease and crime. To many observers, the existing social order seemed to be falling apart.

During the changes that marked the first half of the nineteenth century, the familiar rhythms of the country were replaced by the din of expanding cities. People became more mobile, and the old ways of doing things rapidly changed. The essential relationships that tied people to one another were redefined.

BOX 1.2: COMMUNITY

Community can be defined as a distinct group of people who share connections, characteristics, or needs. These may include geographical space, social position, cultural beliefs, religion, occupation, or any other common set of values or interests that distinguishes their group from the larger society.

The most common definition of community is the people living in a specific (geographical) location. With the development of transportation and communication technologies, the geographic definition of community has become less dominant as new forms have emerged such as communities of interest, comprised of like-minded people who may or may not live close to each other, and virtual communities formed by people who meet and interact online in cyberspace.

Questions were raised by the social thinkers of the day about whether community (the thing that binds people together and gives them a sense of belonging) was dying out. Ordinary people also began to question whether the new social arrangements were better or worse than the ones they had before. Political and academic debates raged about how to deal with the problems created by the rise of cities. It is within this context that the concept of community has played a central, if elusive, role in the development of Western scholarship. It is a key issue in discussions about the nature of social order, social stability, and the processes of social change.

Writing in the late nineteenth century, Émile Durkheim considered the consequences of the rapid changes taking place in the society around him, including the growth of cities and the slow demise of small rural towns and villages. One of his concerns was the nature of social order and the way that it influenced behaviour. He claimed that the breakdown in social order was due to a lack of shared values, which he characterized as normlessness (1964). During periods of rapid social change, people become unsure of the rules (or norms) that guide social behaviour. This results in ANOMIE, a reflection of the loss of the stability and solidarity that typified rural life where everyone knew the rules (the norms) and how they were supposed to act (their roles). However, rather than despairing at the changes and the social problems they engendered, Durkheim posited that urbanization and differentiation, among other factors, were leading to changes in the nature of the ties that connect people to one another.

Durkheim pointed out that smaller, more homogenous groups were held together by common norms and values resulting in what he called MECHANICAL SOLIDARITY. This form of social order was based on strong family ties, shared values and beliefs, and widely understood norms, and it was being challenged by the rise of urbanization and the increased differentiation it created (i.e., the greater number of roles in society, including specialized jobs). However, he believed that a new basis for solidarity was possible based on the new types of social relationships to which people living and working in cities were exposed. He pointed out that they had to depend more and more on strangers to meet their everyday needs. Rather than produce their own goods, they bought their food, clothing, and other necessities from city stores and shops. And rather than working with family and friends, they became part of a large urban workforce organized around different crafts and trades. These workplace organizations provided the opportunity for the development of new kinds of connections based on the common experiences and interests of the workers.

Durkheim was optimistic about these emerging connections and felt that they could replace those that formed the basis of mechanical solidarity. The developing society could find stability in the interdependence that marked urban life in a new form of social order he called ORGANIC SOLIDARITY. In this type of situation, people play many different roles and have different experiences, but they are connected to each other by their need to work and live together, that is, by their interdependence. Durkheim did not use the term community in discussing either of his typologies, but both seem to reflect the way that people relate to each other in complex social relations. In many ways, these relationships mirror what many of us think about today when we think about community.

Perhaps the most famous commentary on community is found in the work of Ferdinand Tönnies (1955[1887]). Writing near the end of the nineteenth century, Tönnies also reflected on the impact of urbanization and industrialization on society. While Durkheim characterized this change as going from mechanical to organic solidarity, Tönnies described it as a shift from GEMEINSCHAFT (community) to GESELLSCHAFT (society). A community, or *gemeinschaft*, is characterized by informal social relationships and the shared values that connect people and hold groups together. By contrast, *gesellschaft* refers to social relations that are less intimate and more impersonal, based on formal rules and regulations governing appropriate behaviour. Tönnies went further, however, asserting that these two ways of organizing communal relations are polar opposites and that the community form is more desirable. In his more pessimistic assessment, he laments the loss of community and its replacement with a world where people's orientation to one another is more formal, impersonal, calculated, and lacking in true emotional connectedness. In mourning the loss of the village community, Tönnies ignored the fact that some were not ideal places for everyone and could, in many ways, be stifling and unpleasant places in which to live. He also failed to recognize that a society based on the *gesellschaft* type of social relations might provide a wide range of benefits that are absent in smaller villages.

The positive image of a small, rural community as painted by Tönnies reflects a nostalgic view—one that accentuates the positive aspects of community while ignoring most of its negative features. Perhaps not surprisingly, such notions continue to exist today as people yearn for a better life and so romanticize images of living in a place where people care for each other and live in harmony with

BOX 1.3: WELCOME TO CELEBRATION, FLORIDA

Over the years many people have tried to create an idyllic community. But as Tom Leonard of MailOnline, found out, this is not easy to do. In an article entitled "The dark heart of Disney's dream town: Celebration has wife-swapping, suicide, vandals ... and now even a brutal murder," Leonard looks at the reality behind Celebration—a model town that was the dream child of Walt Disney who sought to establish a utopian community. And it looks picture perfect. But

> Celebration's reassuring exterior could not hide the unseemly passions of ordinary life forever. Locals like to joke that they live in 'The Bubble,' but that was noisily punctured last week when Celebration recorded its first murder. Less than a week later, the town was rocked by a second serious incident when an armed man barricaded himself into his home. After a 14-hour stand-off with police, 52-year-old Craig Foushee, a former airline pilot who was deeply depressed following his divorce, loss of home, and the failure of his security business, shot himself. His wife had recently accused him of assault. The Christmas red ribbons festooning every other bush in Celebration were joined by yellow police tape. The little children's train that chugs through town suddenly found itself upstaged by the police tank that was brought in with a SWAT team to surround Mr Foushee's home ... Some complain that Celebration's wholesome exterior hides a suffocatingly 'incestuous' community which is rife with divorce and where neighbours even resort to wife-swapping to relieve the boredom. (Leonard 2010)

their neighbours. The modern stereotypical image of such a community can easily be found in movies and literature. It involves a quiet, tree-lined street with large individual homes with front lawns and white picket fences. Life in such a place is imagined as being much simpler and more cohesive than that found in large, impersonal cities. However, as noted, life in small communities has its own challenges, and such idealized notions may be little more than wishful thinking.

What is clear is that urbanization and industrialization resulted in significant shifts in social relations. Social theorists from various points of view noted that different forms of social relationships, and with them different forms of community, were emerging and that these opened up some possibilities while foreclosing others. These new social relationships were ways of coping with urbanization and industrialization and allowed for the maintenance of social cohesion and social order. This challenge was especially difficult given the social ills associated with the rise of cities. While theorists such as Durkheim and Tönnies identified potentially new ways for people to relate to each other, the ways people actually met their needs remained an open question. For example, whose responsibility was it for caring for the needy in urban areas where traditional familial and community supports were absent?

These challenges were met in a variety of ways in cities as the nature of the social support system changed. Early on, support for the needy was a matter of private and individual charities that were designed to address the immediate needs of the beneficiary and to reflect the virtue of the benefactor (Valverde

1991). However, charity of this type was not dependable since it was impulsive and at the whim of the donor. In the emerging urban centres, new structures were required to meet the needs of those unable to manage on their own. Slowly, organized charities and philanthropic societies began to emerge. They sought to rationalize aid and teach those in need (the poor and destitute) the skills of industry, thrift, and self-reliance considered necessary to succeed in the city.

These activities helped shape what has come to be known as THE SOCIAL, that is, the programs and services that people come to expect from the society around them (Valverde 1991). Today, we take a wide variety of state-provided programs and services for granted. These range from the infrastructure that facilitates our daily lives (water, sewers, waste disposal, public utilities) to those that make transportation and communication fast and reliable. It also includes publicly funded education and health care as well as supports such as welfare, public housing, old age pensions, unemployment insurance, and worker's compensation.

BOX 1.4: THE SOCIAL—CANADA'S SOCIAL SAFETY NET

"The social" is the realm of activity in a society through which social support programs and services are provided to its people. They reflect the minimum standards that people in any particular country associate with being a citizen of that country. In Canada, publicly funded health care and education are considered to be the right of all citizens, and these programs form the heart of the social in this country. The package of support programs is referred to as the social safety net, and in addition to health care and education includes such things as welfare, old age pensions, and worker's compensation. It is important to realize that these support programs were not always provided by the state. In fact, most were fought for by generations of Canadians who felt that citizens of a wealthy country such as this should be able to share in its prosperity. Especially after the ravages of the Great Depression, people began to believe that all citizens deserve to live in dignity and be afforded a minimum standard of living whether they can earn it themselves or whether they need public assistance. However, the social safety net is not a panacea or a picnic. This is especially true during the current period of neoliberalism when there have been considerable cutbacks in spending on social programs and services.

> Social assistance originally was intended as Canada's income program of last resort. Its purpose was to provide income when all else fails—when a household has few or no earnings or other sources of income and limited assets…. For some Canadians in need, the myriad welfare rules make it difficult to qualify for benefits even though they face dire economic straits. Those who actually get on the program often encounter problems when they try to move off. They face a veritable "welfare wall." … Still other Canadians remain on the social safety net for much of their life. Their circumstances give new meaning to the concept of life support. Typically, these are persons with severe and prolonged disabilities who live in a society and workforce that simply makes no place for them. The last resort is their first—and sometimes only—option. (Torjman 2007, 1)

The idea behind the growth of the social was that people had some basic rights as members of a society and that the state should be involved in guaranteeing these rights. In particular, it emphasized that social problems that could have an impact on people's lives should be addressed through the collective efforts of the population and through the actions of the state.

While a discussion of the emergence of the social is beyond the scope of this chapter, it is important to note that people fought for these rights—they were not simply granted. Struggles over worker's rights, including workers' compensation, often resulted in bitter confrontations, such as the 1919 Winnipeg General Strike (Kolko 1963; Bercuson 1990). Many of the rights we now take for granted were the result of protracted efforts that saw social problems eventually become defined as everyone's responsibility and that provided a clear and specific role for the state. For example, the current debate in Canada over health care is vastly different from the one taking place in the United States: Canadians fought for and implemented universal, state-funded health care in the 1960s, but the Americans did not, with the result that today over 30 million Americans have no health insurance.

The development and widespread acceptance of the notion of the social was accelerated in most Western democracies during the GREAT DEPRESSION when the state took on a much larger role in the economy than it had in the past. Massive state expenditures were implemented to put people back to work and to restart the faltering economy. The enormous amount of pain and suffering caused by the Great Depression and concerns about the threat of communism led the state to adopt a dramatically changed role from the LAISSEZ-FAIRE approach that had dominated until then. This approach held that the market was self-correcting and that the state should not intervene in the economy. However, during the depression, the market failed to resolve the economic crisis and most Western nations experienced a prolonged period of economic stagnation characterized by massive unemployment, increasing poverty and social unrest. Support began to grow for an expanded role for the state including providing funds for social support programs such as social assistance and employment programs. This approach has come to be known as the KEYNESIAN WELFARE STATE, named after the British economist John Maynard Keynes (1883–1946).With the advent and growth of the welfare state, the social quickly spread beyond the economy (such as employment programs) to address other areas. State agencies and some philanthropic organizations worked to provide increasingly professionalized care to people throughout the course of their lives from cradle to grave. The provision of these social supports came, over time, to be viewed as the responsibility of the state. People began to take for granted that the state had a role in helping them meet their basic needs and to support those most vulnerable to exploitation and harm. At the same time, taking responsibility for providing these supports made sense to central governments that realized that providing social support, especially in times of crisis and need, contributed to political and social stability.

What happened to the community during the period that witnessed the birth and expansion of the social? Carson argues that communities (defined as people with close connections who care for one another) persisted even after the state took on the responsibility for providing key social supports. In fact, he states that communities continued to be important sources of care and support for their members even during this period of dramatic social change. He notes that the shifting face of urban life led "to new groupings, new forms of neo-tribalism centred around temporary forms of solidarity and political organisations" (2004, 10).

For Carson, the community retained important functions even during the period of increasing state involvement in the provision of social support. However, he argues that the nature and role of the community changed as people came together to make new communities under new circumstances. One example of this type of change can be seen in the way the definition of community has increasingly moved away from its primary association with a geographic or spatial location to encompass newer, symbolic forms based on shared values and interests.

Creed (2006) identifies STRUCTURAL DIFFERENTIATION as the critical force that separates community from place and location. Structural differentiation is the result of a combination of factors that includes immigration, population growth, competition for resources under conditions of material density, changing technologies, new systems of production, market mechanisms of distribution, and new forms of consolidating power.

The new communities of the industrial era were based on a commitment to shared values or ideas as opposed to fixed geographical locations. As these communities organized, they began to make their own claims on the social. Their members demanded more rights while seeking to limit the ability of the state to interfere too much in their private lives. For example, racial and ethnic groups, feminists, gays, lesbians, and seniors (among others) came together during the 1970s to mobilize for social change. These symbolic COMMUNITIES OF INTEREST challenged the status quo and especially the welfare state's taken-for-granted provision of supports and services. The very idea of the welfare state came under increasing scrutiny. Criticisms were raised about the way a range of groups, including those seeking assistance, were being treated by the state. Concerns were also expressed over the invasion of privacy and the blatant paternalism that accompanied the provision of such state-administered social supports as welfare and unemployment insurance.

By the mid 1970s, the criticisms of the welfare state approach had grown pervasive. Not only were welfare state policies and programs criticized on ideological grounds (lack of client rights, privacy issues, etc.), they were also becoming too costly for the state to sustain. Raising the funds necessary to pay for the existing level of social support contributed to what O'Connor (1973) describes as the

---

BOX 1.5: WHY IS NEOLIBERALISM SO IMPORTANT?

On 5 August 1981, President Ronald Reagan fired over 11,000 striking air traffic controllers who refused to follow his order and return to work. He did not stop there, however, and ordered a lifetime ban on rehiring these federal employees. This fundamentally changed the rules of the economic game in the United States. Similarly, in the United Kingdom, Margaret Thatcher also challenged organized labour by refusing to give in to striking miners. This led to a bitter and often violent 11-month strike, which ended with the miners returning to work with little to show for their efforts. She essentially broke the union.

Reagan and Thatcher ushered in a new era of political and economic philosophy and practice that marked an end to the welfare state policies that had predominated in Western nations since the Great Depression. In their place, the new approach favoured free market policies, the cutting of public expenditures on social services, deregulation, privatization, and an emphasis on individual responsibility. This approach and underlying philosophy have come to be known as neoliberalism. Countries that adopted this approach moved away from welfare state policies and practices to promote smaller government and a limited role for the state in people's lives. Many of the programs that had come to be taken for granted under the social safety net of the earlier welfare state era were reduced or eliminated as lowering taxes and balancing budgets became the focus of neoliberal governments around the world. The result was reductions and cuts to government-funded health care, education, social services, welfare, and public housing, and the downloading of responsibility for these programs and services to lower levels of government (provinces/territories and municipalities) and onto individuals themselves (in a process known as responsibilization). The consequences for the poor and those least able to meet their own needs have been significant. But the story is not so straightforward nor one-sided. Despite the adoption of a neoliberal approach in Canada and elsewhere, many aspects of the former welfare state remain intact since no political or economic philosophy is able to completely sweep away the vestiges of the previous system. At the same time, people living and working in communities have developed a wide range of responses to neoliberal policies and practices ranging from submission, to resistance, to appropriation and recasting. The result is an amalgam of creative strategies that show that people often do what it takes to make sense of their own situations despite the wishes of local, provincial, or federal authorities.

"fiscal crisis of the state." Serious budget imbalance resulted as social welfare costs increased at the same time that the economy was faltering and interest rates were skyrocketing. In order to secure the funds needed to pay for its social programs, the state could either borrow money (at very high interest rates) and add to the national debt or increase taxes that many argued were already too high and hurting the economy. Disenchantment with the welfare state and demands for change grew, culminating in 1980 with the election of Ronald Reagan in the United States. The like-minded Margaret Thatcher had come to power in May of 1979 in the United Kingdom. These two politicians shared a completely different view of the role and responsibilities of the state than the one based on Keynesian principles and practices. Their new approach has come to be known as neoliberalism.

With the ascendency of Reagan and Thatcher, the very idea of the social was challenged. Indeed, Thatcher (in)famously stated in 1987 that:

> I think we've been through a period where too many people have been given to understand that if they have a problem, it's the government's job to cope with it. "I have a problem, I'll get a grant." "I'm homeless, the government must house me." They're casting their problem on society. And, you know, there is no such thing as society. There are individual men and women, and there are families. And no government can do anything except through people, and people must look to themselves first. It's our duty to look after ourselves and then, also to look after our neighbour. People have got the entitlements too much in mind, without the obligations. There's no such thing as entitlement, unless someone has first met an obligation. (Thatcher 1987)

Questions were raised about whether the state had any responsibility for providing anything but the most minimal social supports. Some observers wondered whether the social safety net had outlived its usefulness. Thus, in 1996 Nicholas Rose announced "the death of the social," killed by the emergence of neoliberalism and the pressures of GLOBALIZATION, with profound consequences for society. Indeed, the death of the social implies for Rose, as it did for Thatcher, that in the end people are responsible for themselves: they are connected to one another only in transitory ways that reflect the types of relationships that characterize social life in a global economy. Most now live as isolated individuals, largely detached from the bonds of community as well as the kinship that characterized an earlier age.

The demise of the social has reverberated throughout society and influenced many of the ways people interact. For example, Putnam (2000) has noted a sharp decline in volunteering and participation in the political process. He argues that this has had a very detrimental impact on the quality of life in American communities. Carson (2004) also argues that political participation is waning and that more and more people are choosing not to vote. In many Western nations, religious participation has also been on the decline. For example, Voas and Crockett (2005) reviewed British social surveys and concluded that there has been a continuous decline in religious observance in the United Kingdom throughout the twentieth century. This has been reported in other Western nations as well. In Putnam's (2000) view, people seem no longer to need or have faith in the institutions that have framed society for the past thousand years. In previous eras, the institutions of civil society, such as the family and the church, represented an important counterbalance to the power and role of the state. With the decline of these institutions, there are fewer layers that can mediate between the individual and the state, resulting in a much more precarious relationship between the two than existed in the past.

If the social ceases to exist, if people have lost faith in social institutions, what happens to community? Interestingly, the concept has become increasingly visible in political and social discourse. It is often romanticized and elevated to a focal point in the discussion of current social arrangements. Alternatively, it is critically assessed and dismissed despite its importance and political cachet (Defilippis et al. 2006). Importantly, though, the community has gained considerable stature in social discourse as it has been appropriated by a wide variety of actors for diverse and often contradictory purposes. Thus, the concept is invoked by people at opposite ends of the political spectrum as well as in relation to things few would associate with community. Consider, for example, that the adjective "community-based" has been used to describe drug treatment programs being offered to inmates in a federal penitentiary because those providing the service say they are dealing with the "prison community." Such a notion, on the surface at least, appears absurd, a long stretch from the commonsense notion of the term typically associated with a geographic location (Stohr et al. 2002).

Why does the concept of community have so much political cachet and broad popular appeal? The answer is at once both simple and complex. Invoking the notion of community immediately suggests that something is local and familiar as opposed to distant and strange. It conjures up a host of positive feelings and images as well as a sense of nostalgia—a yearning for something from the past that is "remembered" as being simpler and more wholesome than life today. Whether such a golden age ever existed is debatable, but this is not the issue. Rather, invoking the community is important for symbolic reasons in so far as it offers a way for people to respond to the anonymity, isolation, and lack of connection that characterizes much of modern social life (Bauman 2001). In this context, community is understood as something that is inherently good and desirable in comparison to other social institutions and processes that are thought of as cold, impersonal, bureaucratic, and largely distasteful.

The popular appeal of the concept of community is akin to the way the term "natural" is currently being used in some advertising to promote various products. Natural implies that such products are wholesome and good in direct opposition to those that are artificial and, by implication, dangerous. Unfortunately, as many consumers have discovered, natural products can be just as harmful as artificial ones. Snake venom is natural, but no one would claim that being bitten by a poisonous snake is not harmful. Yet, at the same time, venom is used to make powerful, live-saving medicines.

And so it is with community. Some aspects of community—what Putnam (2000) calls "bonding social capital"—can have very positive effects by bringing people together in close-knit groups that help and support their members.

However, as he points out, this type of bonding also has a "dark side" since it can lead, in certain circumstances, to the exclusion of outsiders and can promote decidedly undesirable outcomes. For example, both the Ku Klux Klan and the Mafia are groups with high levels of bonding but they are also problematic and anything but wholesome (Putnam 2000, 22). So, as we consider the question of the community, we need to recognize that while it has popular appeal and potential benefits, it is not a panacea for all that ails us.

Defining the Concept of Community

The discussion thus far has been general in nature and skirted the central issue, namely, what do we mean by community? Unfortunately, there is no one single definition that is widely accepted (Bauman 2001; Etzioni 2000; Caputo et al. 2001; Crawford 1999; Kumar 2005; Rose 1999; Schofield 2002). In fact, there are so many competing definitions that some social thinkers have suggested abandoning the term altogether (Etzioni 2000). Day (2006) describes it as one of the most vague and elusive concepts in sociology. The common and extensive use of the word in popular discourse, however, makes ignoring it undesirable and as a result, various authors have offered their own definitions of the concept, which have met with varying degrees of acceptance. The following discussion will help define the key elements associated with the concept of community.

One common usage of the term refers to geographical space, although this can include locations as diverse as a village, a town, and even a city (Caputo et al. 2001, 9), making some researchers reject it altogether and turn instead to the place-based notion of neighbourhood. One reason for this decision is to avoid confusion since the concept of neighbourhood is much more definable. As well, it reflects the way social life is organized for many people on an intimate scale; in an urban centre, for instance, a neighbourhood is an area of about a quarter of a mile in radius with a population of 5,000 to 6,000 people (United Way 2007, 10; Meagher n.d., 11). It is a place where people can walk around comfortably and interact with others during the normal course of everyday life, visiting stores, the post office, schools, churches, parks, and so on (Levitan-Reid 2006, 5; Maclennan 2006, 1). The appeal of such a spatial definition of community is bolstered by the fact that it also often reflects administrative districts, including such political and service delivery boundaries as municipal wards, police districts, or health service areas.

An equally common use of the term retains Tönnies's understanding of community, which emphasizes common interests, values, and beliefs. Etzioni, for example, suggests that communities are based first on "a web of affect-laden relationships among a group of individuals, relationships that often crisscross and reinforce one another (rather than merely one-on-one or chainlike individual

BOX 1.6: EXPLORING THE MEANING OF COMMUNITY

The image that comes to mind when we think of community is the neighbourhood in which we live. Children are often proud of being able to name the streets that surround their homes. They know the location of local shops and services as well as the schools in the area. The importance of this definition of community, based as it is on geography and space, becomes apparent when people meet someone new. Often the first question asked is "Where do you come from?" followed by inquiries about where they grew up or what school they attended. Information such as this provides shorthand clues about the person through stereotypes about various places in the city or country. We can all recite something about the reputations of different neighbourhoods near where we live. In fact, where people live can form an important part of their identity. They can be proud or ashamed depending on whether the neighbourhood is highly regarded or thought of as being less desirable and on the proverbial wrong side of the tracks.

However, this definition as a geographic or spatial location is only one of the ways in which community is defined. Another is based on having shared values or common interests with others. Some examples are the arts community of writers, visual artists, dancers, actors, etc.; the medical community of doctors, nurses, pharmacists, paramedical workers, etc.; and communities based on ethnic or religious affiliation. These can be local, provincial, national, or even international groups who share the same interest or focus. Their members don't have to live in the same neighbourhood or even the same town/city or province.

There is one final twist to this story that makes defining community today even more challenging than it was in the past. The tremendous growth of the Internet and the use of social media has highlighted the emergence of yet another definition of community. Virtual communities include people who meet and interact online on sites such as Facebook and Myspace and in a whole host of virtual spaces such as Second Life, Whyville, and Kinsaki. In these latter sites, people create life-like avatars for themselves who interact with other players in virtual communities. What does community mean in this context? Can we all be members of global communities as a result of our access to the Internet? What consequences does this have for how we define community?

These are just some of the questions to keep in mind as we explore the meaning of community and its implications for the social policies, programs, and practices that influence peoples' lives.

relationships)" and secondly on a measure of commitment to "a set of shared values, norms and meanings, and a shared history and identity—in short, to a particular culture" (Etzioni 2000, 188).

Turner and Dolch (1996) move us even farther away from geographic space by arguing that as a result of changing technology that has made communication and transportation easier and faster, communities are much more fluid now. They are essentially symbolic in nature, and people do not have to be in close proximity to share common symbols and meanings. Virtual communities found on the Internet and the widespread use of social networking programs such as

Facebook and Twitter have resulted in new ways of mobilizing people and supporting collective action. This sense of community has considerable resonance. Consider how social networking was used to organize and share information about the 2010–11 demonstrations in Egypt, Tunisia, and Algeria.

Larner argues that a spatial definition of community does not capture its core element. She integrates the ideas put forward by Etzioni, and Turner and Dolch:

> [T]his community is not simply a geographical space, a social space, a sociological space or a space of services, although it may attach itself to any or all such spatializations. It is a moral field binding people into durable relations. It is a space of emotional relationships through which individual identities are constructed through their bond to micro-cultures of values and meanings. (Larner 2005, 13)

Community here is imagined as the connections between people and the moral attachments that bind them together. In this conceptualization, the social is re-imagined—we no longer agree or are bound together within a society, but there exists within and across national boundaries durable relations that bind us one to the other.

Fettes shares Larner's sense of connection but adds a dynamic role for the individual in being part of and building community:

> I want to propose that community consists, in essence, of such connections between expressed thought and lived experience: a dynamic cyclical relationship between the stories people tell about themselves and the ways they relate to one another and to their environment. It is a definition focused neither on kinship, nor on place, nor on mind, but on the relationships that they exemplify. Kinship exemplifies ways of being together; place exemplifies ways of being in the world; mind is not a passive state but an active process of building, maintaining, and revising shared meanings. Thus the material for building community is ever present, wherever people are and whatever they are doing. (Fettes 1998, 263–64)

These definitions illuminate a core feature of community for most people. They also reflect an ongoing sense that despite widespread social and technological change community remains possible—though its features may change.

These competing definitions of community make it a difficult and confusing concept to understand. As Kumar (2005, 275) notes, the "current focus on community is haunted by the conflation of quite different meanings, by confusion of an ideal type with empirical instances, and by the tendency toward simplification." Further, in thinking about community and how it is defined, we need to consider the impact of the definition of community on the lived experiences of the people to whom it refers. In this sense, whether the reference is to geographical communities or communities of interest, a major question involves identifying who is or who can be a member of the said community and how this membership is determined. These questions raise issues related to identity, democracy, engagement, and exclusion, which are beyond the scope of the present work, but which should be kept in mind.

While the emergence of new definitions of community in changing social conditions is an important development, the increasing focus by the state on community reflects its interest in making communities responsible for the provision of social programs and services. In this context, the community becomes more narrowly defined and its geographical dimension comes to the fore.

How community is defined has an impact on who is considered to be a member. For example, under a geographic definition, one can be a member of a community and not know or even want this, since membership involves simply living there (in a neighbourhood) without requiring that one identify oneself as a member of the particular community. Further, when community is viewed as a geographic area where the state is delivering or has oversight of service delivery, people who work there (as volunteers or professionals) are identified or can claim that they are members of that community. Further, these professionals are often invested with the authority to speak on behalf of the community at meetings where decisions that affect the community are made. Their community membership is presumed, and there is no critical engagement with the fact that they may work for organizations that have their own agendas, goals, and values.[1] In this sense, what does it mean when someone describes a program, service, or agency as community-based?

Such issues are important not only for our understanding of the concept of community, but also impact on its use by the Canadian state as a core element of social policy. Much work done at a local level in this country is described as community-based even in cases where no actual community residents are involved. Further, choices are often made regarding who is accepted as members of the community in question. A variety of groups can legitimately claim to represent the community—but not all such groups will be successful. Finally, the community does not speak with one voice. As Kumar (2005) notes, different advocates can have quite differing ideas about who and what the community is and what it needs. If communities are recognized by the state as geographic entities or only as the professional actors working in (and perhaps on behalf of) the community, if groups the government does not recognize as community go

---

1 Agencies may indeed be part of a community and well able to speak on its behalf. McGrath et al.'s (2007) research on social development practitioners serving four different communities (Aboriginals, gay/lesbian/bisexual/transgendered, immigrants, and refugees) viewed their work as social justice. Though constrained by a variety of features of the political landscape, their work was clearly for and supportive of their constituent communities.

unheard and unheeded, and if state actions ignore the divisions within communities and the role (which many researchers identify as critical) that people have in defining and shaping communities, then the impact of state policies on the community are likely to be complex and contradictory.

Community and Public Policy

It is important to understand how community is understood and used by policy-makers since the concept has become the focus of an increasing number of state policies. Rochefort and his colleagues raise this question when considering how policy-makers use the concept of community as a policy instrument. They note that "community policy instruments are depicted as methods by which government typically seeks to minimize its problem solving, service delivery, and financial responsibility for a given set of social needs" (Rochefort et al. 1998, 549). They go on to point out that the use of community as a policy instrument has many attractions for policy-makers—it is cost efficient and consistent with the cultural norms of Western societies that value community ties. Thus, governments invoke the term community because it appeals to people—it carries the connotation that something is good, wholesome, and responsive to local needs—and because it allows them to reduce their financial responsibility for meeting those needs.

The use of the concept of community within the policy realm, however, is not simple. Rochefort et al. (1998) argue that the term is used in a wide variety of ways even within a single policy domain. For example, community-oriented action may be used to refer to the provision of services outside of an institutional setting. Community may also be used to designate a geographic area in which service is provided and whose members are eligible to use or access that service. It may also be used as a target for intervention; thus, policies are directed at intervening in a location (perhaps through educational programs) and with a particular population to prevent problems from emerging (e.g., students at risk of illicit drug use). Community may also be a setting for service delivery, as it provides a setting that normalizes experiences. But perhaps most importantly, invoking community as a policy instrument provides "an ideological framework for legitimizing diverse system changes, including expanded professional and paraprofessional involvement, ... new roles for citizens in the management of [the] local, and a redefinition of the problem" (Rochefort et al. 1998, 561).

Each of these ways of using the community as a policy instrument makes it an appealing tool for the state. Depending on the specific goal, the concept can be used to set the agenda, to define or redefine problems, and to legitimate what services are provided, where they are provided, who can provide them, and who has access to them. It is also useful in managing what are often complex and challenging relationships with other levels of government, including constitutional divisions of power. Thus, while funding for infrastructure (roads and sewers) is a provincial and municipal responsibility, the Canadian federal government can intervene directly at the municipal level and bypass provincial jurisdiction by transferring a percentage of the gasoline tax it collects to local municipalities. This example has been repeated in a number of other sectors in which the federal government has chosen to steer despite the fact that it does not have the formal jurisdiction to do so.

Using Community Agencies as "The" Community

As we will see in subsequent chapters, community-based agencies have become the FACE OF THE COMMUNITY for many government programs and services as responsibility for managing local concerns has increasingly been downloaded. In the policy realm, these front-line organizations are often called upon to define needs and deliver programs in and on behalf of communities. This has occurred despite the extensive research that defines community as connections among people and shared values. Are agencies, and their staff, members of communities, and do they truly represent the community?

The picture is even more complicated because priorities and programs are determined externally, since the state has the power to set the agenda and control the resources needed to act. Turner and Martin (2003) described this as an approach in which the state does the STEERING while the community does the ROWING. In this formulation, a community of connected individuals is absent.

The use in social policy of agencies (in the place of residents or those with a value and/or moral connection to the community) as the community has significant implications for community agencies and residents alike. Orsini (2006) describes this as HOLLOWING OUT of the community. This involves a reduced role for community members in a process whereby agencies and organizations are physically based in communities but are no longer run by the residents of these communities: "[r]ather than being a peoples' movement, community groups now represent a movement of groups with specialized mandates defined by government priorities, rather than representing a movement defined by citizens' needs" (Orsini 2006, 32).

These agencies have their own *raison d'être* including values, mission statements, and financial considerations that may not be consistent with the interests or needs of others in the community, including other service providers. They have professional staffs and boards of directors who reflect a range of political and economic interests. For many of these organizations, securing state funding is crucial to pay for staff and programs. As a result, the relationship of community-based organizations with the communities they serve is often complicated as they have to "tailor their agendas to the needs and priorities of the state" (Orsini 2006, 24). Failing to do so may have a profound impact on their ability to continue to operate.

Thus, when community-based organizations are accepted by the government as the community, they must, if they seek government funding, respond to government directives to support their agencies' existence. This makes funding a key aspect in shaping what happens on the ground. For example, through its funding programs, the government determines priority groups and concerns. Orsini (2006, 33) argues that some agencies, including those that engage in advocacy work (such as women's centres) receive less funding than groups providing services or serving groups the state sets as a priority. In the Canadian context, the focus has often been on health and on priority groups such as seniors and young children. The funding priority process creates dilemmas for front-line agencies whose programs assist marginal groups. They are faced with either refusing funding and not having the resources they need for their programs or pursuing funding that addresses the needs of the priority groups identified by the state.

This situation exists partly because the community that is imagined in state policy is a generic one (Kumar 2005) that does not exist in reality. Rather, it is constructed through the process of policy enactment. The selection of groups to represent the face of the community, however, is the manifestation of what are defined as real communities. This raises a number of important concerns. For example, Orsini (2006, 25) argues that groups who receive funding are required to "navigate a complicated maze of government policies and practices to qualify for support." State oversight may make participation unappealing and mechanisms such as audits that require detailed client information may limit groups willing to participate. Smaller organizations may not have the capacity to apply for funding or meet the requirements to administer it in a way that conforms to state expectations. This effectively limits who applies for funding and who is considered as a representative of the community

Is the Community Able to Act?

In addition to identifying who can act on behalf of the community, the state has to identify communities that have the capacity to take on this role (Turner and Martin 2003). Having the capacity to act involves leadership and the ability to mobilize resources. It also requires that individuals in the community are willing and able to participate in community-based activities, including delivering services.

There are a number of concerns related to the ability and capacity of a community to act. The interest (both of the state and of agencies within a community) in getting communities action-ready has led to the development of a variety of tools and other resources for assessing community readiness, documenting community assets, and building **COMMUNITY CAPACITY**.

To create communities that have the ability to meet local needs requires that a variety of individuals be willing to get involved; this includes professionals and paraprofessionals (such as the staff of not-for-profit organizations) as well as local residents. The move to the community has had a significant impact on a wide variety of actors at both the state and community levels.

Consider the case of community policing in which the police and the community are supposed to work together to identify and respond to community safety concerns. This represents a new and different approach for the police who had the sole responsible for public safety in the past. As part of a community policing strategy, everyone in the community is implicated and responsible for acting to make the community safe by stopping or preventing crime. This responsibility ranges from putting in alarm systems to participating in Neighbourhood Watch initiatives and to making sure doors and windows are locked. We are now all responsible for our own and for our community's safety—this is no longer the sole responsibility of the police. But can we act? Do we have the resources to protect our homes and ourselves? Enhancing security systems and buying better locks takes money, which we may or may not have. Even crime prevention strategies that may not require a lot of money to operate, such as Neighbourhood Watch, require some resources. In order to organize such a program, a community must have considerable capacity. There must be someone to lead and organize the initiative. There must be a place to hold meetings and a way of contacting people to participate. Further, there must be an interest or willingness to participate. In some communities—especially those where residents have limited incomes or live below the poverty line—there may be no resources in the neighbourhood, and so there is no Neighbourhood Watch. Alternately, in neighbourhoods that have mixed groups—such as privately owned residences and public housing projects—the owners of the private residences may have the ability and resources to organize and will develop a Neighbourhood Watch for their local area. They may also view their neighbours in public housing as the problem, thus creating distrust and hostility between those involved and protected and those not involved. So, there are issues around the ability and capacity to act and issues around who is acting and in whose interests.

Bringing Community Back In

Questions about how we define community have important implications for the role this concept has come to play in the context of the rise of neoliberalism in Canada and in other Western nations. The popular appeal of the community has been seized upon to legitimate various practices including the downloading of responsibility for programs and services from the state level to the local level. However, the power to set the agenda, to define priorities, and to control resources has remained with the state. Those groups and voluntary or non-governmental organizations that have historically provided services on behalf of the state in communities have had to adapt to the new steering role of the state in order to survive. This has included competing for funding and being subjected to increasing scrutiny and accountability.

The impact of these developments and their consequences for both those living and working in communities forms the subject matter for the remainder of this volume. We will explore the move toward the community in various sectors in Canada and discuss the implications this has had on communities and especially for those working at the community level. We begin by considering the emergence of neoliberalism and the implications of downloading responsibility to the local level on the provision of social services and programs. The emergence of neoliberalism is considered in a broad historical context, highlighting both the developments that led to the demise of the welfare state and how neoliberalism has been used to alter the nature of existing social relationships in Canada and other Western nations. As part of this analysis, a number of case studies will illustrate how the changes ushered in by neoliberal regimes in Canada have made a real difference to what goes on in communities across the country. In particular, we look at the impact of these changes on the people who work at the community level in the countless agencies and organizations that provide programs and services to thousands of ordinary Canadians. We conclude by considering the implications that these changes have for the future of communities in this country.

Chapter 2

WHY COMMUNITY? WHY NOW?

Introduction

Why have we experienced a shift to the community? Why has it occurred now? To answer these questions requires an understanding of the political and economic developments that marked the last decades of the twentieth century and that continue to influence government policy today. In this chapter we examine neoliberalism—an approach to both governing and the economy that emerged in a variety of forms in the 1970s in most Western democracies and many developing nations—with a primary focus on its impact in Canada.

It is important at the outset of this discussion to recognize that there is no single definition of neoliberalism since neoliberal policy and practice has varied across nation-states and over time. Thus, while there are a number of underlying principles and a body of theory related to neoliberalism, the practices that governments follow adhere to these ideals in varying degrees. Despite these apparent differences, however, the term is often used as if it represents a cohesive and consistent set of ideas and practices. In reality that is not the case. Rather, nation-states following a neoliberal approach have produced a variety of "neoliberalisms" based on their history and culture as well as their social, political, and economic circumstances.

The neoliberal turn—that is, the emergence and development of neoliberalism—has been global in its scope but local in its impact. As states have deregulated, divested, and reduced or eliminated the services they provide, the impact of these actions has been felt most pointedly by people living and working in local communities. For example, some observers have argued that the neoliberal policies that resulted in the DEREGULATION of food inspection laws in the province of Ontario contributed to the outbreak of listeriosis in that province in 2008. The lack of government inspections and inspectors allowed the contamination to go unchecked for a lengthy period, resulting in 19 deaths and numerous people getting sick (Curry and Fenlon 2008). A similar situation precipitated the crisis in Walkerton, Ontario where seven people died and hundreds became seriously ill from drinking contaminated water as a result of the deregulation of provincial environmental laws coupled with cutbacks in the number of inspectors responsible for water safety and their lack of training and supervision. A public inquiry into the incident blamed the crisis on cutbacks introduced by the Progressive Conservative government of Mike Harris. As Snider (2004, 268) notes: "The O'Connor Report, published on 14 January 2007 blamed government policies for allowing the disaster to happen. It particularly criticized decisions to decimate the Ministry of the Environment and redefine regulation as mere communication with stake-holders."

As these examples show, it is important to ground the consideration of the impact of the neoliberal turn in Canada by examining how neoliberal policies and practices have been adopted in this country (including deregulation and cutbacks to government agencies such as the Ministry of the Environment) and the impact these changes have had at the local level on the lives of ordinary Canadians.

Defining Neoliberalism

Neoliberalism emerged in the 1970s, eventually becoming a dominant political philosophy around the world. As David Harvey (2005) notes:

> There has everywhere been an emphatic turn towards neoliberalism in the political-economic practices and thinking since the 1970s. Deregulation, **PRIVATIZATION**, and withdrawal of the state from many areas of social provision have been all too common. Almost all states, from those newly minted after the collapse of the Soviet Union to old-style social democracies and welfare states such as New Zealand and Sweden, have embraced, sometimes voluntarily and in other instances in response to coercive pressures, some version of neoliberal theory and adjusted at least some policies and practices accordingly. (Harvey 2005, 2–3)

Neoliberalism, like community, is a much used term. At its root, it is a theory about capitalist markets and the role of the state in **CAPITAL ACCUMULATION** (Harvey 2005). Neoliberal theory argues that capitalist markets are self-correcting and, if left to their own devices, will produce the best possible economic outcomes. Problems emerge when markets are hampered by government regulation, government ownership, and other intrusive government policies such as social welfare spending on, for instance, publicly funded education and health care. While neoliberalism is a theory about how markets function and the limited role the state should play, it is also about the political-economic practices that states should follow to ensure the optimum operation of markets and the concomitant accumulation of wealth.

Defining neoliberalism is challenging because it has assumed a variety of forms at different times and in different nation-states. Further, states regarded as neoliberal often have features that are simultaneously both neoliberal and not neoliberal. This has led some commentators to reject the concept of a single neoliberalism, making the concept more challenging to define. Hackworth and Moriah (2006, 510), for example, note that:

> [W]hile it is clear that neoliberalism is influential within contemporary urban political economy, it is not at all clear that what many identify as "neoliberalism" is a coherent theoretical, political, or geographical project. Many have suggested that neoliberalism is either too internally riven with contradiction to be considered a singular ideology (Brenner and Theodore 2002; Gough 2002), or that its implementation is so locally contingent that we cannot plausibly speak of one ideal-type placeless neoliberalism (Mitchel 2001, 2004; Keil 2002; Wilson 2004). There are, in other words, many differences of viewpoint in how neoliberalism is defined, and how it manifests locally.

In spite of these differences, it is necessary to define the broad premises of the philosophy behind the approach in order to understand the community-based shift and its consequences. Neoliberalism is "an economic doctrine which gives supremacy to free markets as a method of handling not only the economic affairs of nations, but also a political ideology which can be applied to all manner of governance issues" (Hartman 2005, 58). Understanding this definition and its implications requires an appreciation of the history of state intervention in the economy.

The Political Economy of State Intervention

In the 1930s the Great Depression posed a serious threat to the capitalist system. The problem and challenges of this global depression were addressed, in part, through the restructuring of states and their international relations. The aim was to create the right blend of state, market, and democratic institutions that would ensure economic stability. The core element of determining this right blend was defining the appropriate level of involvement of the state in "achieving full employment, economic growth, and the welfare of its citizens" (Harvey 2005, 10). Based, initially, on the theories of British economist John Maynard Keynes, the state was encouraged to do this by intervening actively in the market. In order to get people back to work and to reduce the threat that widespread

BOX 2.1: THE GREAT DEPRESSION

"The Great Depression was ushered in by the stock market crash of October 29, 1929. It ended as dramatically a decade later on September 3, 1939, when the Second World War began. The widespread poverty and suffering during the 1930s—the result of unemployment, drought, and lack of a social safety net—transformed social welfare in Canada.

Until the 1930s, mainly private charities dealt with unemployment and poverty. However, charity work was usually organized to meet temporary or seasonal crises, such as poor harvests or fires. This approach could not cope with an economic crisis the length and intensity of the Great Depression. Although the federal and provincial governments were completely unprepared, they intervened and made care of the poor, sick, unemployed, and disadvantaged a high priority.

During the 1930s, the unemployed received uneven treatment across Canada. Married men or men with families were favoured over single men and women when relief or relief work was distributed. Many cities established residence requirements to keep out job seekers from other provinces or towns. To help spur an economic recovery, the federal government increased its spending on relief, subsidies and work camps, among other things. This resulted in a ballooning national debt" (Statistics Canada 2008).

unemployment posed, governments around the world began to intervene in the economy to a much greater extent than they had before. Many used state funds to provide an economic stimulus that could spark the stagnant economy back to life even if this meant running large budget deficits.

The Great Depression put millions of people out of work. Typical of the era are images of long soup lines and of people riding the rails and living in hobo camps. The economic solutions of the past were clearly not working and something had to be done to rectify the situation, given the widespread misery the prolonged recession had caused and the potential for a complete collapse of the economic system.

Mass spending by the state on employment programs was only one of the steps taken. For example, income support systems such as welfare, unemployment insurance, and old age security were developed or expanded. Regulatory systems were also put in place to govern such things as health and safety, taxation, and trade policy. The specific nature and extent of the emerging social support systems varied from state to state, but overall the result was that "market processes and entrepreneurial and corporate activities were surrounded by a web of social and political constraints and regulatory environment that sometimes restrained but in other instances led the way in economic and industrial strategy" (Harvey 2005, 11).

By the end of the 1960s, the Keynesian welfare state was beginning to unravel as economic conditions worsened once again. Nation-states were increasingly

BOX 2.2: BROTHER, CAN YOU SPARE A DIME?

In general, Depression-era songs were encouraging, telling people to look on the bright side and that things would get better. "Brother, Can You Spare a Dime?" was different—it spoke of the real misery and need experienced by ordinary people.

Most Broadway songs began talking about the difficult times, but

instead of finishing with weary resignation from the Depression, [this song ends an] octave higher, with a fortissimo. We've gone from depression to hope. We've gone from depression to hope in the first verse, and we finish with anger. And although the first two times were 'Brother, Can You Spare a Dime?'—a kind of harmless brotherhood of man—it finishes with 'Buddy, Can You Spare a Dime?' We don't finish with any 'Life is a bowl of cherries.' We're finishing with the anger of the two socialist creators, Gorney and Harburg, always feeling the time-immemorial complaint that the working man doesn't get the rewards. In the middle of the Depression, in 1932, when no one was saying this out loud, they had the courage to say it on Broadway. (NPR 2008)

unable to afford the kind of spending on social benefits begun during the Great Depression. This led, as we saw in the previous chapter, to what O'Connor (1973, 6) called "the fiscal crisis of the state." In order to pay for social programs, nation-states could either increase taxes, run deficits, or do both. These strategies, however, led to soaring interest rates as states borrowed more and more money to pay for social programs and to service their massive debts. Rising tax burdens put increasing pressure on both businesses and consumers, resulting in economic stagnation and growing unemployment.

As Hartman (2005, 62) notes, "the apparent failure of the welfare state—high inflation, the oil crisis of 1973, and high unemployment rates—all contributed to an economic climate in which governments, citizens, and capitalists were open to finding an alternative way to deal with the problems." The proponents of neoliberalism offered an approach that appealed to more and more people as the fiscal crisis deepened. This does not mean that neoliberalism was inevitable, but it was clear that the welfare state approach that had been the status quo for over 30 years was not working and that a new approach would find support in this turbulent economic climate.

Minimizing the Role of the State

Neoliberalism is based on the monetarist ideas of economists Friedrich von Hayek (1899–1992) and Milton Friedman (1912–2006). Both critiqued state intervention in the market and argued that the role of the state "should be limited to securing private property rights and contracts" (Hartman 2005, 59). To achieve this, the state should shift as many costs as possible back onto individuals, barriers or restrictions on competition should be eliminated, and the tax burden on market agents should be reduced. Thus, in Canada:

> Proceeding from the premises of monetarist economic theory, neoliberalism introduced a sweeping series of measures to widen the scope of markets in social life. These included deregulation, privatization, regressive tax reforms, erosion and dismantling of social services, campaigns of state deficit- and debt-reduction, the opening of doors to foreign investment, and attacks on trade-union rights. What the policies of neoliberalism have in common is a commitment to "the principle of corporate private property, and its defence and advancement" (Teeple 2000, 6)—a commitment whose rationality seems self-evident in a context of heightened international competition, not only among firms but among states seeking the new investments that power local economies. (Carroll and Shaw 2001, 196)

In addition to these specific changes, Miller (2007, 226) notes three basic trends in the development of neoliberalism. First, he argues that state responsibilities have been reorganized so that various functions have been downloaded to local levels while regulatory functions have been retained by the national government. At the same time, local states (provinces/territories and municipalities) have been pitted against each other to compete for capital investment. Second, many formerly public institutions and services have been privatized, with a concomitant change in decision-making that replaced democratic models with those that prioritize the market even in the social services sector. Finally, "there has been a triumph of market ideology: the notion that markets are the best, most efficient, and socially optimal means of allocating scarce resources *in virtually all realms of life*" (Miller 2007, 225; emphasis added).

A number of observers have attempted to classify periods of neoliberal development. One of the most prominent is Peck and Tickell's (2002) identification of "ROLL-BACK/ROLL-OUT NEOLIBERALISM." Roll-back neoliberalism dismantled the Keynesian welfare state's institutions and practices. In the roll-out phase, alternate means of meeting needs are introduced, including making local groups and agencies (communities) responsible for dealing with the challenges of providing services to those in need. Further, as the negative impacts of roll-backs become evident, the state constructs a variety of mechanisms for addressing the resulting concerns. Throughout this process, the state maintains its control by introducing a variety of techniques, including requiring those receiving state funds to submit to greater EVALUATION and accountability requirements. As well, key regulatory functions are uploaded from the local to the national state level. These mechanisms are part of what has come to be known as the NEW PUBLIC MANAGEMENT, which allows the state to continue to manage an increasingly decentralized provision of programs and services.

Neoliberalism in the Canadian Context

The neoliberal turn in Canada began federally with the coming to power of the Progressive Conservative government in 1984. It introduced a series of changes that reflect the deregulation and privatization themes discussed above. They were followed in office by the Liberal Party, which continued and expanded its own version of the neoliberal approach throughout the 1990s, especially in relation to taxation and social spending:

> In the last decades, the Canadian welfare state has been dwindling. The Liberal Party government's (1990–January 2006) commitment to deficit reduction, economic growth, and international competitiveness has brought about health, education, and welfare spending cutbacks. Economic restraint led to the weakening of Canada's social safety net (Olsen 2002). The present Conservative Party government [led by Stephen Harper] is poised to take very similar social policies to those of the Liberal Party, perhaps even more neoliberal. (Tang and Peters 2006, 572)

Mahon (2005) notes that in addition to the cutbacks, responsibility for social services has been downloaded from the national to the subnational level, especially where responsibilities for many key social programs (including health and education) are shared by the federal, provincial/territorial, and, in some cases municipal governments. This shared responsibility is evident in the distribution of power and responsibility as well as in the nature of the political-economic philosophies of the subnational governments that jealously guard their constitutionally defined powers and areas of responsibility (Harmes 2007). Thus, while the actions of the federal government have been important during the neoliberal turn in Canada, the role of provincial/territorial and municipal governments must also be taken into account.

It is also important to bear in mind that in Canada the vestiges of the welfare state remained visible during the period when neoliberal policies and practices were enacted. The intricate mixture of roll-back and roll-out policies that have altered the political and economic landscape of the country have been built on the existing foundation of welfare state institutions and practices. While an attempt to dismantle the welfare state is evident, not all of its structures and processes have been eliminated. In many respects, it continues to have some sway in both public expectations (what people have come to expect from their governments)

> **BOX 2.3: A DISGRUNTLED SENIOR CITIZEN
> —PRIME MINISTER MULRONEY MEETS SOLANGE DENIS**
>
> "1984–85 ... In an attempt to curb ballooning government spending, Mulroney makes drastic cuts that lead to difficulties in keeping election promises. A government plan to limit inflation protection on Old Age Security pensions leads to a much-publicized ambush on the front steps of Parliament, when 63-year-old Solange Denis tells the prime minister, 'You made promises that you wouldn't touch anything.... You lied to us. I was made to vote for you and then it's goodbye, Charlie Brown.' The government later backed down on the proposal." (CBC News In Depth 2007)

and government policies and practices (how the bureaucracy works and what politicians promote). For example, while people may support tax cuts, they also expect a wide range of services to be provided by the state. Similarly, while politicians may espouse a neoliberal philosophy, few are willing to make serious cuts to **"SACRED" SOCIAL PROGRAMS** for fear of a massive public backlash. This happened on 19 June 1985 to the Mulroney Progressive Conservative government, which quickly backed off its plans to cut old age pension benefits when an animated senior citizen, Solange Denis, challenged the government on the steps of the Parliament buildings.

Given the often contradictory array of programs and strategies introduced by successive Canadian governments, is it possible to identify the key features of Canadian neoliberalism? The short answer is yes. In practice, neoliberalism here has led to such things as the privatization and commodification of public assets, including telecommunications, energy (Petro-Canada, for example), water, transportation, and education. In addition, there has been a roll-back of regulatory frameworks that protected labour and the environment. There have also been changes to taxation policy and cutbacks in state expenditure in areas such as employment insurance, pensions, welfare, social housing, and health care. Importantly, the extent of privatization, deregulation, and cutbacks to social support services has varied across the country, depending on the history and political cultures of each region or province.

Habibov and Fan (2008) provide a detailed analysis of the neoliberal changes that have altered the nature of the Canadian social safety net, including income security, old age security, the Canada/Quebec pension plan, unemployment/ employment insurance, family benefits, social assistance, and other income transfers. In general, they report that "total inequality in Canada considerably increased throughout the 1990s, while the effectiveness of the income security system decreased" (2008, 34). With respect to old age security, they note that what had been a universal program was changed in 1991 with the introduction of an income test that saw benefits gradually reduced for seniors above a certain level of net income. Old age benefits were also slightly reduced as a result of changes to how the Canada/Quebec pension plan benefits were calculated. There was also a reduction in disability benefits, and a maximum limit was established for death benefits.

Moreover, significant changes were also made to the unemployment insurance system. This key component of the social safety net was designed to protect people who lost their jobs, but it also provided insurance for sickness as well as maternity and parental benefits. The federal government passed the Unemployment Insurance Act in 1940 to create a national system of unemployment insurance financed through contributions by the federal government, employers, and employees. Successive neoliberal governments dramatically altered the unemployment insurance program throughout the 1990s (Habibov and Fan 2008). For example, the name of the program was changed from Unemployment Insurance to the Employment Insurance (EI) program. This subtle name change, however, does not reflect the more significant changes that were made. The program is now entirely funded by premiums paid by employees and employers with the federal government cancelling its once significant contributions. Silver et al. (2005, 33) note that other modifications such as "raising the benefit qualification requirement, reducing the benefit rate, and completely disqualifying workers who quit 'without just cause.'" They go on to state that since these changes were implemented, the use of EI has fallen and almost half of the people who are unemployed are not eligible for the program. Thus, the impact of neoliberalism on those facing unemployment has been dramatic:

> Changes in EI reflect a neoliberal belief that compensation for the unemployed is bad for the labour market because the unemployed will be less willing to accept a job and the employed will be more willing to quit (Atkinson and Micklewright 1991). The privatization and individuation of the unemployment safety net has forced many of those ineligible for EI to move back with their parents, live on savings, seek help from friends and relatives, or apply for social assistance (Crompton and Vickers 2000). (Silver et al. 2005, 33)

Like unemployment insurance, family benefits have also been an important part of the social safety net through the use of family allowance and refundable tax credits. Both were universal programs intended for families with children, and in 1989 both benefits were cancelled for wealthier families. "Both programs were abolished during the reforms in favour of the Canada Child Tax Benefit that was designed as an income-tested program delivering benefits through the income tax return system and fully funded by provincial and federal budgets" (Habibov and Fan 2008, 36).

These changes to family allowance tell only part of the story, however, as can be seen in an examination of the support provided to single mothers with dependent children, who traditionally have been defined as deserving of social support in both Canada and the United States. The American Social Security Act of 1935 and the Canada Assistance Plan (CAP) of 1966 both granted income support to single mothers as a basic right of citizenship. Even though the benefits were not always adequate, nor always granted, they did provide support to a vulnerable and needy population. However, with the advent of neoliberalism in the 1990s, policies in both countries changed, and the nature of state support for these women was dramatically altered:

> In 1996, the US Aid to Families with Dependent Children (AFDC) was replaced with the Temporary Aid for Needy Families (TANF) under the Personal Responsibility and Work Reconciliation Act (PRWORA) (Korteweg, 2006). In a similar manner, the CAP was replaced with the Canada Health and Social Transfer. Both of these policy changes involved a transformation in social spending arrangements between levels of government and so provided the economic rationale to curtail entitlements to support and reduce benefit amounts (Corcoran et al. 2000; Bashevkin 2002) in the hopes of reducing caseloads and associated costs. (Gazso and McDaniel 2010, 372)

The very name of the American legislation—the Personal Responsibility and Work Reconciliation Act—says a great deal about the mood of the day. Gazso and McDaniel go on to point out that in the case of women with dependent children in Canada, "income support programmes based on rights of social citizenship became scapegoats for mothers' presumed dysfunctional work ethic and unconventional family structures ..." (2010, 372).

For many in need, social assistance represents a last resort, but social assistance programs were also restructured as a result of neoliberal polices. These programs were administered by provincial governments according to national standards and through a cost-sharing arrangement with the federal government, which contributed 50 per cent of the funding. Habibov and Fan list many of the drastic changes that were made to this important component of Canada's social safety net—changes that reflect both the substance and spirit of neoliberalism:

> After the reforms, the cost-sharing agreement and national standards were abolished. Stringent measures were taken to decrease the number of recipients. The benefit level was reduced, and case reviews and fraud investigations increased through the employment of additional monitors and extensive home visits. Furthermore, special telephone "snitch lines" were set up and citizens were encouraged to report fraud, while benefit recipients were required to take their benefits in person. Assets previously exempted from the calculation of benefits, such as life insurance policies, interest earned on liquid assets, and the increase in value of a home while the owner was on welfare, were now

WHY COMMUNITY? WHY NOW?   33

included in the computation of entitlements. Recipients in common-law relationships were no longer eligible to apply for benefits as a single person or lone parent. Real values of benefits decreased. Recipients were also required to participate in various workfare activities ranging from active job searches to unpaid community work; those who refused to participate in workfare or abandoned a job without a good reason were ineligible for the benefits. (2008, 36)

The changes ushered in by successive neoliberal governments also struck at what most Canadians consider to be the heart of their social safety net—the publicly funded health care system. Cutbacks resulted in massive changes, including a chronic lack of beds, backed-up emergency rooms, and long wait times for various medical procedures. Health care expenditures are one of the largest budget items for both the federal and provincial governments, and the crisis in health care has been at the centre of an ongoing debate about how to fix the ailing system. Not surprisingly, neoliberal supporters have called for the introduction of various reforms based on market-oriented solutions such as privatizing health care and introducing a user-pay system to make people more responsible and improve the efficiency of the system.

In her analysis of the health care issue, Heather Whiteside (2009) argues that the question is less a problem of efficiency than of how the economic system works and specifically how capital accumulation occurs. The collapse of the economic system during the Great Depression marked the failure of the capitalist system to achieve sufficient levels of capital accumulation. The adoption of the Keynesian welfare state approach provided one type of solution to the problem of accumulation. Neoliberalism offers another. Whiteside raises a note of caution, however, about the neoliberal response when it comes to the provision of social supports such as publicly funded health care:

Neoliberalism poses serious challenges to any social service more suited to the KWS [Keynesian welfare state], and medicare is especially vulnerable.... The adoption of neoliberalism has resulted in a two-front assault on [the publicly funded health care system's] processes and principles. First, deep funding cuts and freezes on future increases during the 1980s and 1990s dramatically challenged its functioning. Second, the more recent adoption of public-private partnerships (P3s) and the privatization of support services increasingly commodify its future development, undermining its core tenets. (2009, 81)

These changes have resulted in serious challenges to the functioning of Canada's publicly funded health care system. Given the widespread concern this has caused, it is not surprising that health care is at the top of the political agenda in Canada with competing voices offering their own particular version of an appropriate fix.

Nor has publicly funded education in Canada fared much better. As another major social program, it also represents a key budget item for both federal and provincial governments. Like income security programs, unemployment insurance, social assistance, and health care, cuts to education spending have been dramatic during the rise of neoliberalism. For example, during the 1990s alone, successive federal Liberal governments cut funding for education by $5 billion through reduced transfer payments to the provinces. At the same time, some provinces were promoting privatization in the education field by creating tax credit schemes designed to encourage people to seek private educational services. Davidson-Harden et al. conclude that "education indicators for the country as a whole show—particularly during the nineties—an overall decrease in basic secondary and postsecondary education funding per student (Statistics Canada and CMEC 1999) ..." (2009, 52–53).

Not all of the changes brought about by neoliberalism have been so straight-forward or one dimensional. In many cases, a mixed bag of outcomes has left people on the ground trying their best to make sense of the changing environment. For example, Hackworth and Moriah (2005) studied the result of cutbacks and restructuring in the 1990s to social housing policy in Ontario, which led to a large increase in homelessness and a crisis in the social housing sector. The federal government intervened by providing $300 million for social housing across the country—an offer that was contingent on the provinces and territories matching the funding. The Ontario Progressive Conservative government of Mike Harris, one of the most profoundly neoliberal in the country, refused to invest in affordable housing, arguing that housing markets were best left to market mechanisms rather than government intervention. As a result, they declined to act, and the funds went unused until a Liberal government came to power in the province. Not only had homelessness dramatically increased, but:

> The second, perhaps unintended, consequence of social housing restructuring in Ontario has been the creation of an institutional kaleidoscope that is difficult to navigate for even the most seasoned housing provider. The downloading of responsibility for housing units once held by the federal and provincial governments has been an institutionally complex matter.... The increase in complexity and the decrease in expertise is an ironic one, as the ostensible intent of downloading, and restructuring more generally, was the absolute reverse (to decrease complexity and increase expertise by localizing responsibility). A third, largely unexplored, consequence of social housing restructuring has been the creation of a space for experimentation, primarily amongst non-profit housing providers and municipalities in the province, resulting from the downloading of responsibility to local officials. This "space," argue some, holds great promise (for creating more affordable housing) but also contains much danger for the

further privatization of the stock and the development of a highly uneven system like that of the US. Much remains to be established about how non-profits are operating within this context. (Hackwork and Moriah 2005, 516)

This analysis suggests that neoliberal policies do not have universally negative or positive outcomes. The landscape facing local groups and organizations responding to social needs is affected by state policy; however, the way communities respond is not completely determined by what the governments intend. Thus, while neoliberal governments at both the federal and provincial levels have had an impact on communities, the outcomes have proven to be complex, unintended, and often contradictory.

Basu's (2007) work on the closing of Ontario schools under neoliberalism provides another example of the local response to neoliberal policies. Various techniques were used by local groups including outright refusals to identify any schools for closure, seeking to delay closures, developing bargaining strategies to keep schools open (such as projecting significantly higher bussing costs), and arguing that demand for schools would grow based on the area's demographics or proposed new development. Different situations resulted in some communities being much more effective than others in organizing and successfully challenging state policy.

Beres et al. (2009) provide another example of resistance to neoliberal policies in their study of sexual assault/rape crisis centres, which rely extensively on provincial funding and the unpaid voluntary labour of women. During the rise of neoliberalism, there were massive budgets cuts by the federal government to programs supporting women, including "decreased funding for antiviolence initiatives." At the same time, "federal government actors mounted a steady rhetorical attack on the women's movement, delegitimizing feminist voices and dismantling programs designed to enhance women's equality" (2009, 142). Provincial governments followed suit, and funding for women's centres was reduced and state agencies devoted to women's equality were eliminated. In the face of such a powerful onslaught, it would be easy to assume that those responsible for running women's centres would have little choice but to acquiesce to the neoliberal agenda and forego their advocacy role if they wanted to continue receiving state funding. This, however, has not been the case:

In sum, our data indicates that despite significant pressures to redefine as victims' service agencies, Canadian SAC/RCCs [sexual assault/rape crisis centres] continue to see themselves as agents of social change; many embrace feminist principles of organizing, and most engage in diverse forms of social/political/ feminist activism to raise awareness about sexual violence and fight for its elimination. (Beres et al. 2009, 152)

Resistance to neoliberal attacks on women's programs also occurred in British Columbia after the provincial government introduced policies that resulted in "shifting public programs and services away from equity and support [so that] local-level workers [found] themselves relatively powerless to stem the tide of change as attempts to resist change at the local level met with limited results." In response, women's groups went to the United Nations to challenge the changes, because Canada was a signatory to the United Nations Convention on the Elimination of All Forms of Discrimination against Women. "Recently, the committee determined that the Canadian government (including the British Columbia provincial government) had violated the Women's Convention when instituting massive cutbacks and called upon the Canadian government to redress the situation" (Tang and Peters 2006, 571–72).

What is particularly important about these examples is that they document the complex outcomes that flowed from the introduction of neoliberal policies. At the local level, a variety of techniques were used to respond to policy changes with some communities being much more effective than others in adapting or resisting the changes. Basu's (2007) analysis, for example, indicates that parents with more wealth, prestige, and status were better able to prevent their schools from closing. At the same time, the research conducted by Beres et al. (2009) and Tang and Peters (2006) shows how women's groups were able to resist the impact of neoliberal policies by working at the local level as well as by mobilizing international support.

As this brief overview of the Canadian experience with neoliberalism has illustrated, there has been a profound shift in the role of the state with respect to the provision of programs and social services. This shift has been marked by a growing reliance on market-based solutions with the market being prescribed as the corrective mechanism for all social ills. However, the impact of neoliberalism is neither total nor linear. Both positive and negative outcomes have been reported, with many groups and organizations adapting in their own ways, including active resistance.

The manifestations of neoliberalism in Canada continued unabated from the early 1980s until the global financial crisis of 2008. The federal Conservative government of Stephen Harper initially advocated staying its neoliberal course even as the global financial collapse led many Western nations—notably the country's biggest trading partner, the United States—to take drastic action and begin massive spending campaigns in order to stimulate economic activity. Both the enormous level of state spending and the huge budget deficits it caused fly directly in the face of accepted neoliberal orthodoxy. In fact, massive state expenditures to stimulate a flagging economic system is a strategy that harkens back to the welfare state approach developed in the 1930s in response to the Great Depression.

As the global financial crisis deepened in 2009, the Harper government was forced to abandon its neoliberal orientation—tax cuts, balanced budgets, and deficit reduction—and engage in large-scale spending of its own in order to avoid having the country fall deeper into recession. This resulted in huge budget deficits, which are anathema to the political orientation of the government and of the prime minister in particular. At the same time, rather than let the market deal with failing corporations, the government provided large amounts of public funds to bail out faltering businesses, including several large automobile manufacturing corporations. Once again, the state had to step in to preserve jobs and support a fragile economy. Both of these actions would have been unthinkable just a few short years before. Nevertheless, it was clear that a neoliberal fix could not solve the problem.

What happened to the community during this neoliberal period when dramatic changes were made to social support programs? The responsibility for many programs and services was downloaded from the federal state onto lower levels of government and eventually onto the community. At the same time, the federal government introduced a number of mechanisms designed to allow it to retain control over regulatory rights as well as over the funding process. The following section provides a more detailed examination of some of the mechanisms used by the state to retain control over the way social support programs and services are designed and delivered.

Neoliberalism and Community

One of the most profound changes ushered in through the neoliberal turn has been the downloading of the responsibility for social support programs from the state to the community. In many countries, including the United Kingdom, the United States, Australia, New Zealand, and Canada, services previously provided by the state—even those it offered in institutional settings (mental health, services for the developmentally delayed, etc.)—have been transferred to community settings. At the same time, other services that had been funded for years by the state were eliminated. In some cases, new and more limited programs were introduced to replace some of those that were cut. As part of this process, the state provided funding to various individuals, groups, and organizations in the community for the delivery of particular services.

The move toward the community under neoliberalism allowed the state to divest itself of costly social programs and services through cutbacks and the transfer of responsibility to others, thus minimizing the role of the state while emphasizing that individuals should be responsible for their own well-being. The state justified downloading as supporting more direct democracy since community programs would ostensibly be controlled and delivered by local groups and individuals, which would make service delivery more efficient.

An important consideration in the move toward the community has been how to provide services that are necessary and useful but that cannot generate a profit and, therefore, cannot be left to market forces. There are many public services that enhance the quality of life of citizens but do not generate profits. Police and fire protection, waste management, and the upkeep and maintenance of public parks and public buildings are only a few examples of the many services that are paid for with public funds and for which there is no expectation of making a profit. Outsourcing some of these services to private firms and replacing government employees with contract help would still not turn them into profit-making ventures. In some cases, states have moved to a user-pay system that charges people for the level of services they use (e.g., charging by the bag for garbage collection). However, this logic cannot be applied to all public services since some are simply not amenable to such an approach (can you imagine charging people for visiting a local public park?).

How can the state get its citizens to accept more of the responsibility for meeting their own needs, especially in the case of programs and services that cannot be run for a profit? The ideological thrust of the neoliberal approach is that the state should play a limited role in society. Taxes should be kept to a minimum as should the state's involvement in society and especially the economy. The corollary of this proposition is that people should be required to take care of themselves and their own needs. Getting the public to accept these ideas is the subject of much of the ideological discourse surrounding the development and expansion of neoliberalism.

Getting people to accept more responsibility for themselves and their fellow citizens is a process that has been termed responsibilization—the attempt to educate people about what is required of them to be successful citizens (Rist and Humphrey 2010). Responsibilization, in neoliberal terms, is a way of providing benefits to both individuals and to the wider society. Its benefits will be realized as individual assets are harnessed for the competitive advantage of all (Cheshire and Lawrence 2005; Harvey 1989; Levi 2008; Pavey et al. 2007; Rist and Humphrey 2010). When ordinary citizens accept the responsibility for providing programs and services that had once been provided by the state, everyone is seen as benefiting. This is especially true for those services that do not generate profits.

Children's Development Accounts (CDAs) are an example of a responsibilization program developed by the American government. This program, aimed at children in low-income households, assists their families to save money that can then be invested in educational or entrepreneurial training. The goal of this training is to help these children get ahead (Rist and Humphrey 2010). It transfers the responsibility for education to parents by providing them with modest amounts of money that they are supposed to use to purchase the type of education and training that had previously been provided by the state. Moreover, the program is delivered through the community on a not-for-profit basis and is supposedly cost effective since no state employees are involved. More importantly, it shifts the responsibility to support these children as they make their way in the world away from state-run educational institutions and onto individual families and students.

Situational crime prevention programs sponsored by the state represent another example of responsibilization. In this case, the responsibility for keeping people and their property safe has been shifted away from law enforcement authorities onto ordinary citizens. People are encouraged to take on more responsibility for protecting themselves and their property from crime by buying and installing better lighting and stronger locks or hiring private security companies to monitor their property.

Gray (2009) examines how health and safety laws in Canada have been changed in the process of responsibilization. Historically, health and safety laws have focused on the role of employers who have been held accountable for unsafe working conditions. Neoliberal laws have made workers increasingly responsible for their own safety while on the job: "Under the responsibilization strategy of health and safety, workers are not only redefined as both potential victims and offenders, but they also find themselves forced to adopt a rights-defined identity" (Gray 2009, 327). This means that workers have been made responsible for the safety of their work environment: they are the ones who should be asking questions about safety, making complaints, and exercising their rights under the law. The onus for a safe work environment shifts in this way from the employer onto the employees. The changes do not end here, however, as Gray demonstrates through his analysis of a ticketing enforcement strategy introduced by the Ontario government. Both companies and workers in high-risk industries were issued tickets (much like parking tickets) for health and safety violations. However, as Gray points out, "overall, health and safety ticketing falls more heavily upon frontline workers than high-risk employers." More importantly, "workplace safety is undergoing a process of 'responsibilization' as governments reconfigure their role in directions consonant with now dominant mantras of neo-liberal policy. Workers are assigned ever greater responsibility for their own safety at work and are held accountable, judged, and sanctioned through this lens" (2009: 326, 336).

Responsibilization is only one way in which the neoliberal state has tried to deal with its desire to cut state expenditures and get the community (and ordinary citizens) to pick up the slack. Various states have also sought community-based solutions to a variety of issues such as how to care for those who had previously been institutionalized, including the developmentally delayed or those with mental health issues. With the push to cut costs and lower expenditures on social programs and services, many state institutions were closed with the promise that funds would be provided to local groups so that care could be provided in the community. Such promises, however, often went unfulfilled and as Read (2009, 25) notes:

> In British Columbia, thousands of psychiatric patients at Riverview Hospital have been transferred to the community since the 1990s. Although many patients benefit from community integration, some may experience negative effects. Funds saved by this trend have not been allocated to provide necessary supports to mentally ill people in the community. Due to a deficiency in mental health resources, this population is at risk for homelessness, drug abuse, incarceration in jail, and suicide.

Although the mentally ill and the developmentally delayed can be taken out of institutions and put into the community, they still have needs, and their care may include various challenges that have to be met by someone. And if the state will no longer care for them, then their families must. This solution, however, does not fully resolve the situation because the families themselves typically need support and services to do the job properly. In some communities, not-for-profit agencies have become involved since many are willing to do the work in order to get state funding. The work is usually done at a lower cost than when it was provided by the government, but this often masks the fact that social service workers in small not-for-profit agencies often make lower wages and have fewer benefits than those working for the government in similar jobs.

Like families, the not-for-profit sector presents an alternative location for the state to transfer responsibility for programs and services. Working with the not-for-profit sector, however, also has benefits and drawbacks. For example, in an effort to retain some control, the state typically imposes a variety of requirements on the agencies it funds. Levi (2008) describes these as **AUDIT TECHNOLOGIES** and notes that they have a variety of consequences. They serve to harness the potential of these agencies, responsibilizing them through audits and other mechanisms such as required evaluations and the mandated use of **BEST PRACTICES**. In general, the agencies are turned into agents of the neoliberal state and are forced to remain in this role if they want to continue to receive state funding. Many have no other option since they depend on state funds to retain their staff and keep their doors open.

The use of the funding process as a means of controlling various actors such as not-for-profit agencies is discussed in greater detail later in Chapter 5. It is important to emphasize here that the relationship between the state and local actors is not simply one of using funding as a control mechanism. As noted above, those at the community level try to make sense of their circumstances by adapting to the changes around them. Some accept the changes that are imposed, while others vehemently oppose or resist neoliberal policies and practices. Those

---

BOX 2.4: COMMUNITY CAPACITY BUILDING: THE CAPACITY-FOCUSED ALTERNATIVE

"There are two reasons for [a] capacity-oriented emphasis. First, all the historic evidence indicates that significant community development only takes place when local community people are committed to investing themselves and their resources in the effort. This is why you can't develop communities from the top down, or from the outside in. You can, however, provide valuable outside assistance to communities that are actively developing their own assets. The second reason for emphasizing the development of the internal assets of local urban neighborhoods is that there is very little prospect that large-scale industrial or service corporations will be locating in these neighborhoods.... The hard truth is that development must start from within the community and, in most of our urban neighborhoods, there is no other choice" (McKnight and Kretzmann 1996).

---

that accept these changes actively restructure themselves to provide the kinds of services and programs the state is willing to fund, and they use the profits they make doing this to support their traditional activities. There are many examples of this kind of strategy. One involves a large agency serving youth that agreed to take on the responsibility of running a regional youth detention centre and a secure school program even though these two activities were clearly outside its mandate and *raison d'être*. The agency agreed to do this work in order to generate additional income that it could use to support its more traditional work with street-involved youth, youth at risk, and family counselling—none of which are current state priorities.

There are further consequences of the move toward the community. The neoliberal emphasis on responsibilization makes states vulnerable since they have to rely on others. Some states have turned to various control measures in order to address this concern. Others have sought to increase the viability of their community partners by investing in community capacity building. This move recognizes that more is required than simply promoting individual responsibilization in order to make downloading successful. The emphasis on community capacity building has led to a proliferation of asset-based community development programs (ABCD), which argue that individuals and communities have strengths (assets) that can be harnessed to transform both individual lives and whole communities (see Kretzmann and McKnight 1993: Ennis and West 2010).

Even though the focus of community capacity building initiatives is local, the neoliberal state attempts to redefine it as a process that is common to all communities. The state's emphasis on best practices as well as its attempt to generate knowledge, models, and programs that can be transferred from site to site transcends the supposedly local focus of capacity building. Instead, a standardized template is developed, complete with accepted best practice recommendations and detailed prescriptions of how to build community capacity so that it can be replicated from place to place without any reference to local conditions. As Sandler (2007) notes, such an approach fails to recognize the complex roles that social inequality and power play in community outcomes, factors that make the transferability of knowledge and practices problematic at best.

The State Will Steer—Will the Community Row?

As we have seen, the neoliberal turn led successive Canadian governments to attempt to divest themselves of the responsibility for delivering a wide range of social services and programs. This has been dressed in the rhetoric of returning control to the community and as empowering local actors, but one of its main motivations is to reduce the state's responsibility for program delivery. In turning to the community, the state has sought to build communities that are prepared to take responsibility for and respond to local problems, issues, and concerns. The state has also sought to simultaneously download responsibility and retain control over programs and program delivery.

Neoliberal states have developed a wide range of strategies for governing through the community, including how to mobilize community representatives to be in the service of the state. This requires changes to how the state and community-based agencies work together as well as some alteration within the state bureaucracy itself (Bellefeuille and Hemingway 2005). Orsini (2006) argues that these changes have resulted in serious challenges for those working at the community level. While these agencies may be located in communities and provide services there, control over what they do and how they do it has been increasingly usurped by the state.

As noted above, the state has sought to maintain its control over spending on social programs and services by introducing a range of new mechanisms. In addition, it has defined priority funding areas while reducing the overall amount of funding it has made available for social programs. It has imposed new and more stringent funding requirements and gone so far as to require those applying for funding to establish PARTNERSHIPS with others as a condition of getting funding. It has increased scrutiny over those receiving funding through enhanced auditing procedures while emphasizing measurable outcomes through the inclusion of rigorous evaluations. These strategies are, in part, mechanisms that allow the state to set the direction, steer activities, and control the process through which public funds are distributed. While the state is steering, however, the community is supposed to row—that is, the community is supposed to do the work that is required to meet local needs. In this context, the ability of communities to pursue their own interests or agendas, or influence what happens on the ground, is considerably diminished. The strategies that have been developed by the state to steer the agenda are part of what is termed "new public management".

New Public Management

Baines (2006) defines the new public management as an approach to managing projects by requiring agencies to develop quantitative measures of performance goals, benchmarks, and ongoing evaluation. These requirements have had a serious impact on how not-for-profit and voluntary sector organizations provide services, on the activities they undertake, and on the clients they serve. For example, they have been required to expand their documentation and increase their use and reporting of statistics measuring success. Further, outcomes have become increasingly focused on specific, measurable results that have to be achieved within the funding mandate—a timeframe that usually lasts between one and three years. This can be challenging for groups and organizations that are providing services that are intended to have long-term consequences, such as educational programs designed to reduce dropping out of high school but that are delivered during the early years of a student's school experience. The need for immediate and measurable results has made it difficult for groups to get support for programs that focus on long-term outcomes.

As noted above, another key requirement in the new public management strategy has been to require those seeking funding to engage partners for their projects. This process has enhanced the ability of the state to shape what goes on at the local level since it puts a premium on certain kinds of groups or agencies—those that are well-established and more likely to already be going in the direction the state is steering. Requiring partnerships is an arm's-length method for influencing how need is defined at the community level. Only those groups or agencies that are positioned in such a way as to garner partnership support are likely to get funding. This replaces local knowledge and decision-making by forcing those working at the local level to negotiate in an often politically charged funding environment in which every agency jockeys for its share of the available pool of public funds. In such a context, the bigger fish often swallow the smaller ones since they usually have more resources and a greater capacity to meet the enhanced criteria required to successfully compete for public funds. As we will explore later in the book (see Chapter 4), partnerships have become an important issue for groups and organizations seeking to provide services at the community level.

Another key dimension of the new public management is the surveillance of community-based programs through evaluation. Evaluation has increasingly become a key component of state funding as it focuses on identifying tangible results and documenting that these results are due to program activities. It introduces new demands on groups and organizations wanting to deliver programs at the local level and allows the state to review all program activities and ensure that they are delivering the promised and presumably desired results. Further, the success or failure of a program is no longer the responsibility of the state but of the organization delivering it and the community in which it operates. In the process, the state appears to be monitoring activities to ensure that funds are appropriately and effectively spent, thereby obscuring the extensive role it has played in setting the agenda.

Funding

Funding is another major component of the state's steering of community-based activities. To understand this requires an examination of the history of funding practices in order to put the current situation into context. From the 1950s to the 1980s, the Canadian government invested heavily in a wide range of social services. This included both the state's direct provision of services and funding for non-government organizations to provide services. Thus, while the federal government provided many services itself, it also provided funding to a variety of local not-for-profit groups and organizations.

Before the neoliberal turn, organizations received funding based on their mandate, which might include serving special groups (e.g., battered women, the elderly) or the population in general (e.g., the provision of health care information). They were allowed to use the funds they received from the state to support their efforts not only in the actual delivery of services but also for staff salaries and the costs associated with maintaining offices and overhead. Further, the organizations determined how the funds they received were spent. They set priorities based on local conditions and the detailed and expert knowledge of people working on the ground in communities. The organizations had to make a case in order to receive funding, but generally the presence of a population in need was key.

This funding model was termed CORE FUNDING (Gibson et al. 2007; Canadian Council on Social Development 2003). It was based on the provision of financial support to cover core organizational and administrative costs—i.e., salaries for administrative personnel, office space, phone and fax lines, and office equipment—in addition to specific expenses related to program delivery. Core funding covered the costs for people and operational resources that allowed the organization to run day-to-day and to apply for funding not directly related to a particular project or service but to its overall mandate. Thus, it was, generally, long-term funding, and it provided organizations with a relatively predictable way of financing their operations. While funds were provided by the federal government, the planning for service provision was either done in-house or in consultations with the government. The priorities were based on the knowledge and assessment of what was needed locally by the organizations working at the local (community) level.

With the advent of neoliberal funding regimes, the provision of social services and funding for them took a dramatic turn. The state increased its reliance on contracting out to provide many services. In downloading responsibility for service provision to the not-for-profit sector and in reassessing the amount of funding it would provide, the funding mechanisms became a key means the state used for exerting and increasing its control (Canadian Council on Social Development 2003; Gibson 2007). The new funding process has been termed **PROJECT FUNDING.**

Under project funding, the state sets the funding priorities. Instead of providing core funding, they now provide funds for discrete, usually short-term projects. While core funding did allow for some funds to be directed toward rent and administration, project funding cannot. It is not meant to be used to fund the ongoing costs of running the organization providing the services. Funding was tied to the delivery of short-term projects while the funds needed by organizations to survive were eliminated or reduced. In practice, the shift to project funding has meant that local needs are no longer shaping the activities of local agencies. Instead, support is available only for certain groups and organizations and only for activities prioritized by the state. For example, if seniors are a federal funding priority but the local need is for affordable housing for single-parent families, local service organizations face a dilemma. The federal government may not be funding such programs, so the local organizations have to look to other sources for the resources to address the local issue. However, if the organizations are facing a financial crisis and need to bring in some sort of funding to keep their doors open, they would have to make themselves eligible for federal funding by shifting their priority to seniors and not address the need they know exists in the community. Further, if an organization's target group is not on the federal government's priority list, then it may find that it is not able to tap into any federal funding. As well, even if an organization does qualify for funding, this does not usually include the costs associated with keeping it running.

In this type of funding environment, organizations need to develop project proposals that fit into the funding guidelines developed by the state. Many have found this to be extremely taxing since they do not have the resources or capacity needed to constantly develop new proposals and at the same time pay for office space, equipment, and support staff. While all of these things are needed in order to apply for government funding, they are typically not covered under the government funding process. Moreover, since much of the funding is for short-term projects, organizations have to scramble to keep applying for this type of **SOFT MONEY** (as opposed to the core funding provided in an earlier era) in order to keep staff employed. Increasingly, organizations have had to hire people on short-term contracts tied directly to project funding since they have few sources of long-term financial support. This has had serious consequences for the organizations, the people working for them, and the entire social services sector. It has led to insecurity and uncertainty for both those providing and receiving services.

Project funding has other consequences. There is an ongoing competition for available funds. In many instances, groups and organizations from the same community are put in competition with each other as they strive to secure the funds they need to carry out their mandates and, in some cases, the funds they need to survive. During one project, seven of 21 organizations that were participating in a regional initiative on juvenile prostitution were closed within three months of the first meeting of the group. The larger organizations and the state-funded participants (hospitals, schools, police) continued while the smaller, not-for-profit groups had to close their doors. This had a devastating impact on them and the clients they served. However, the remaining organizations were also affected since they were forced to take on additional responsibilities with no new resources. The reality with project funding is that power struggles may emerge where some groups are winners—successful in attracting funds—while others are unsuccessful and may, in fact, cease to exist.

In 2000, the federal government expressed concern over how funds provided to organizations were being spent. In particular, it raised questions about poor auditing of project files from granting programs (Gibson et al. 2007). Once funds were provided, it was assumed that organizations used them for the purposes for which they were intended, but there were no audits of how the funds were spent. Furthermore, the federal government began to increasingly raise questions about the effectiveness of the programs that had been funded.

The federal government responded with enhanced accountability measures. They introduced increased auditing of expenditures and result-based management, an approach that stresses quantitative measures of success (Baines 2006; Gibson et al. 2007; Canadian Council on Social Development 2003). The costs for auditing and assessment were either outside of the program funding or reduced the funds available for program delivery. These auditing and accountability measures have a number of implications. Auditing, for example, may require the sharing of client information with the federal government. For those organizations working with a population such as street youth or new immigrants, privacy issues are important concerns as their clients may be reluctant to seek services from organizations that do not or cannot protect their privacy.

Discussion

The emergence and development of neoliberalism in Canada has had a profound impact on communities, especially with respect to the provisions of social support programs and services. Neoliberal policies have included deregulation, privatization, and tax cuts as well as severe cutbacks to many of the programs that formed the core of the social safety net in Canada. The state has used these strategies in its attempt to move away from the interventionist role of the former Keynesian welfare state approach that had existed for half a century. An important part of this process has been the downloading of responsibility from the national state to the local level. This has been accomplished, in part, through a process of responsibilization in which the state has attempted to instill the notion that to be good citizens, groups and individuals should strive to meet their own needs and take care of themselves.

As part of a broader strategy, neoliberal governments in Canada have changed various laws in order to redefine benefits and the rules under which they are administered. This has excluded many former recipients while reducing the benefits received by others. At the same time, long-standing programs have been eliminated altogether with smaller, more targeted ones introduced to take their place. While downloading responsibility for social programs and services onto local actors, the state has attempted to retain its power to steer the process at arm's length. However, whether the community will row according to the state's steering remains an open question. The implementation of neoliberal policies and practices has been neither linear nor inevitable; several examples above show both acquiescence and resistance to the actions of the state. Thus, in some cases, the community has been willing to row, while in others community groups have refused and vehemently resisted state policies and practices.

In order to manage such a challenging and potentially volatile situation, the state has developed a series of management processes that allow it to retain control over the activities of those in the community working on its behalf. Through the introduction of new public management policies and practices, the state has fundamentally altered how services are designed and delivered, affecting both those providing and receiving these services. Indeed, the actions of successive neoliberal governments have had a profound impact on what happens on the ground in Canadian communities. The actions of the neoliberal state and the strategies it has implemented have important implications for those living and working in communities. Some of these will be addressed in greater detail through the examination of a number of case studies in the chapters that follow.

Chapter 3

IDENTIFYING COMMUNITY—PUTTING THE NEOLIBERAL AGENDA INTO ACTION

Introduction

The previous chapter discussed the emergence and widespread adoption of neo-liberal ideology in Canada and other Western democracies around the world. The rise of neoliberalism signalled the start of a prolonged assault on Keynesian ideology and practice. However, neoliberal states did not have an entirely clean canvas on which to work but, instead, had to deal with the existing welfare state structures and processes. They also had to deal with public beliefs and expectations that had been built up over many years. In practice, each state had to adapt neoliberal ideology, policy, and practice to its own unique social, political, economic, cultural, and historical context. The result in many countries has been an odd blending of the old with the new such that each has its own distinct form of neoliberalism that reflects neoliberal philosophy to a greater or lesser extent.

In Canada, various neoliberal governments have translated neoliberalism to meet their own particular political agendas. They have pursued deregulation, privatization, and responsibilization with a distinctly Canadian flavour. Thus, while there have been cutbacks to many social services and programs, important ones such as the publicly funded health care system remain intact though some critics would argue that it is on life support. And while there has been deregulation in this country, it has not gone nearly as far as it has in other places such as the United States or the United Kingdom where deregulation of the financial sector contributed to the financial meltdown that sparked the global financial crisis of 2008.

It is within this theoretical context that the state moved toward the community to achieve its goals of minimizing its role in the economy, reducing the economic burden of social programs and services, and transferring the responsibility for these back onto ordinary citizens. Indeed, responsibilization is an important strategy in the assault of neoliberal states on the remnants of the Keynesian welfare state and the social. However, as has been the case with the rise of neoliberalism itself, the move by the state toward the community is neither inevitable nor total in its scope. While neoliberal states have sought to steer, the examples explored in Chapter 2 show that the public is not always willing to row or at least not in the way intended by the state. In some cases, people acquiesce and accept the dictates of the state while in others they resist, reframe, or outwardly reject the state's policies and program direction.

An important point to highlight here is that the actions of the state—neoliberal or otherwise—are not undertaken in a vacuum. Rather, they take place in a dynamic, contested, and often controversial context. Understanding what actually happens on the ground requires a critical and nuanced analysis. Developments are rarely simple or linear but reflect the complexities—the give and take—of the world in which they occur. They are often part of an ongoing process rather than a complete transformation, and they are built on the foundation and remnants of what came before, which often influences the results of contemporary action.

This chapter looks more closely at how the theoretical framework presented thus far can help us better understand what happens in communities as a result of neoliberal policies and practices. In particular, we focus on the practical challenges experienced by the state as it has attempted to move toward the local, cut spending, and download the responsibility for social programs and services onto communities. In the process, we explore some of the intricacies related to the concept of community and the challenges that face those working at the local level within a neoliberal policy regime. These include questions related to defining the community in practice as well as issues related to membership and decision-making.

Who Is the Community? Who Wants to Know?

Who is the community and how is it defined? Kumar (2005) suggests that states usually begin with a vision of the community that is generic; that is, the state doesn't have a specific community in mind but rather an idea about what a typical community looks like. Unfortunately, this kind of typical or ideal community does not exist in reality. As a result, the state has to examine the characteristics of real or existing communities and then decide with whom it is willing to work. Not all communities will be suitable candidates for the state. Some may not have the capacity to take on the responsibility being downloaded. Others may be too unstable or unreliable. Thus, the primary issue is the need for the state to define the community. Perhaps more importantly, it has to identify real communities that meet its criteria. This represents a significant challenge in many parts of the country.

Finding real communities with which to work is not an easy task for the state. For example, what definition of community will the state use? Will it rely on the commonsense notion of the community as a geographic entity and use existing administrative or political boundaries? Will it invoke cultural or interest-based definitions of community to meet some local, regional, or even national political imperative? Or will it find other ways to meet its objectives at the local level? There are no easy or simple answers to these questions, and each choice has a set of positive and negative consequences that impact on state/community relations.

An equally important question is who will actually do the work the state wants done and how will these individuals or organizations be identified? The state will have to locate individuals or organizations willing to take on the responsibility of doing the work and who also have the capacity to do the job. What constraints will these actors face and how will they deal with the challenges they may encounter?

Finally, will these individuals or organizations be able to continue to provide the program or service in the long term, after state funding has ended? Many of these programs and services meet basic needs on which people rely for their ongoing well-being. These programs need to be sustainable even if state priorities shift and funding programs end. The state must act carefully if it wants to avoid public displeasure over the termination of long-standing programs and services, thus making the move toward the community a tricky and complicated process.

Thus far, we have talked about identifying community from the perspective of the state. However, it is not always the initiator of community-based programs. Through funding streams and other mechanisms, the state makes money available for community-based initiatives to a wide variety of actors. A group or organization may identify itself as willing to work on behalf of a community and apply for funding. While the state retains a role in the process by specifying funding criteria and establishing who can apply, it may not do much of the work required to identify real communities. Those groups and organizations that apply for state funding may represent themselves as being community-based. Many, however, are typically focused on a specific population, program, or service area. While they may be addressing an issue or group that is important to a particular segment of people, it may be only one of many such issues and groups in a community. To address this, the Canadian neoliberal policy has required that groups and agencies seeking funding must find partners while meeting the needs of specific communities. This sounds like a simple solution, but it poses a difficult challenge since it requires those seeking funding to identify potential partners who are interested in the issue and who are compatible with respect to mandate and ideology. Finding non-profit groups and agencies willing to work in partnership can be difficult since most are seeking funding opportunities themselves or they are already overtaxed and have few resources that they can devote to new initiatives.

Indeed, the competition for scarce resources is considerable in this highly mobile, complex, and heterogeneous society. In such a context, it can be difficult to determine what community-based means when people come together in numerous ways and membership in a community need not be closely associated with where a person lives. As a result, agencies claiming to be community-based may encounter many challenges in attempting to identify a real community with which to work. That is, they may have to search for particular groups of people with whom to align themselves as they address the specific issues that reflect their mandates or interests.

Establishing partnerships, however, is more than simply identifying groups or organizations that are willing to work together. Those seeking partners must also consider what being a partner means and whether potential partners are able to follow through on any agreement that is made. After a long period of cutbacks when many in the non-profit sector have struggled just to keep their doors open, the complexity of entering into partnerships with others becomes a critical issue. In this kind of environment, the challenges facing those groups and organizations seeking state funding and establishing partnerships can be daunting. There is a more detailed discussion of the complexities of partnerships in Chapters 4 and 5 of this book.

In the remainder of this chapter, we examine three case studies that highlight the challenges that face the state as it attempts to enact neoliberal policy. As noted above, the idea of the state moving toward the community is clear and straightforward in theory. In practice, however, it can be fraught with the vagaries that reflect the realities of life in Canadian communities. While the neoliberal state seeks to steer policy, it has to identify a community that is willing and able to row, and it has to ensure that a variety of state and non-state actors are also willing to work within its framework.

The first case study portrays the challenges of identifying a community. It also illustrates that there are some areas of state policy, in this case criminal justice policy, that are particularly resistant to the move toward the community. This resistance reflects the unwillingness of some state actors to forego or give up some of their traditional power and influence. In the second case study, neoliberal policy and practice are in almost perfect alignment. In this example, the state funded a community-based initiative that had the business community as a key partner; together, they adopted a strategy that was consistent with neoliberal philosophy—believing that people should be more responsible for their own well-being and finding mechanisms for funding local initiatives independent of the state. The final case study shows how a community group worked within a neoliberal funding context to achieve its own goals and objectives. In this case, the organization developed partnerships with the police, local government, and other agencies and used them to put pressure on the state to fund what was locally defined as important. Even as state priorities and policy changed, they continued to focus on their local interests and to use pressure to get funding based on this rather than on state priorities.

Case Study 3.1: The Case of a Community-Based Restorative Justice Project

In 2000–01, the authors were involved in a restorative justice project aimed at people living in several public housing complexes in a large Canadian city. The project was funded through a Social Science and Humanities Research Council, Community-University Research Alliance (CURA) grant. These grants were intended to link academic researchers with community-based groups and organizations. The academics were supposed to contribute their skills and expertise in community projects as part of a broader funding regime initiated by the state to support knowledge transfer. In this respect, the CURA funding stream represents a neoliberal approach since it named communities as research partners. While this type of strategy had been going on in business and technology for a long time, it was new to the social sciences, representing a way for the state to shift funds previously earmarked for pure research to a purpose better suited to its own agenda. Making university researchers accessible to communities could help to build community capacity and develop knowledge that could be shared more broadly to support state initiatives. On the other hand, using strategies such as requiring those receiving funding to adopt best practices is an important way of controlling the agenda, since it is the state who decides what constitutes a best practice, and it is the state that has the power to force those seeking funding to use it.

Through the CURA funding stream, the state identified two groups that it recognized as being important actors in community-based activities—university researchers and an "appropriate community-serving agency" (CURA grant application), which meant an agency that had expertise in the area that the project addressed as well as experience in working with communities. In this formulation, the state set the parameters of who could be considered potential community actors in the project. The state followed such an approach in the past when it decided unilaterally who would receive funding for the direct delivery of programs or services. For research funding, however, this represented an important departure from past practice and signalled a new way for the state to direct where and how the funds it provided for research would be spent.

The CURA project provides an interesting example of how the intentions of this funding stream fared when put into practice. The project began when we were approached by a colleague working in a large agency that provides services to high-risk youth. He had learned about CURA funding and thought it was a good way to provide needed services for his clients. He suggested that we apply for funding to start a restorative justice program. We saw this as an interesting opportunity, since restorative justice can be truly community-based in that people from the community can deliver and manage these programs themselves.

In general, restorative justice responds to criminal offences by diverting offenders from the formal justice system through such techniques as Family Group Conferencing, Youth Justice Forums, Victim-Offender Mediation, and Sentencing Circles. The project we were involved with employed Youth Justice Forums. In restorative justice programs, the goal is to repair the harm caused by offenders by having them make reparations to the victim and the community. Then an effort is made to reintegrate the offenders back into the community. The restorative justice process involves the offenders accepting responsibility for their actions in a group setting (a forum, conference or circle). They are required to express remorse, apologize and make restitution. Those participating in the conference or circle offer their forgiveness. The participants symbolically represent "the community" into which the offender is being reintegrated. Forums can be convened and led by community members and while professionals may participate, it is not required. They are intended to be a community-based alternative to the court system.

We began our restorative justice project with a goal of increasing the community's ability to influence the justice system when it came to processing youth from the community. Community members were going to be trained to participate in restorative justice circles, advise us on setting up the program and, in the process, gain a modicum of control over how their young people were treated by the justice system. These goals represent a shift away from a traditional approach that says we should leave justice to the professionals, toward one that promotes increased inclusion of "the community" in addressing/redressing criminal offences. An additional goal of the project was to promote sustainability, that is, to have the restorative justice project continue after the CURA funding ended. This required someone to take responsibility for the project—and that "someone" was supposed to be "the community."

While the idea of starting a community-based restorative justice program was promising in theory, we found it difficult to put into practice. It was challenging to determine a community we could work with. Within restorative justice theory, the answer to "who is the community" is generally non-specific. In practice, the community can be more than people living and working in a particular geographic area. It can include the people who work in agencies and organizations in communities. They may have offices in the community and actually claim to be "community-based" but they still have their own mandates and interests that are separate from those of the people they work with.

In practice, most community-based restorative programs in Canada rely on criminal justice personnel (especially the police and the Crown attorney) for referrals and participation in the process. Indeed, in many Canadian communities, the police have taken the lead by organizing meetings, inviting people to participate, and determining which offenders will be referred to the program. Even where the police do not administer the restorative justice program, they remain in a position of power because they are the ones that make referrals. Without referrals, such programs cannot operate.

In developing a definition of community in our CURA project, we needed to take into account the role of the police and how it would influence our definition of the community. We began with a place-based definition because we wanted to provide alternatives to the formal justice system to young people living in disadvantaged neighbourhoods with high rates of youth crime. However, our original plan had to be changed because the police insisted that they could only make referrals based on police districts. If we wanted referrals, we would have to work within the boundaries of one police district. Since we needed referrals for the program to run, community came to be defined in our CURA project as a geographic and administrative space that coincided with a particular police district. This was the first layer of our emerging definition of community.

Given the parameters imposed by the police, we sought a community that could benefit most from a restorative justice program. We asked for data on the level of youth crime in the various police administrative districts in the city and used this information to determine where there might be youth who could benefit from our project. Based on this assessment, we identified two districts with the highest youth crime rates. In each district there were two high-density social housing projects that the police identified as having a high concentration of calls for service related to youth. In this way, community for our project became defined as a geographic entity, the parameters of which were defined first by the administrative policies of the police and second by the concentration of police contacts with young people in conflict with the law. This became the second level in our emerging definition of community.

Once this initial geographic definition was established, we were faced with a series of issues concerning the people to be included. The first decision was that the community would consist of those living in the social housing complexes identified as trouble-prone. These community residents represented the project's core group. Next, we had to decide on how to define those who worked in the community, including many of the partners who had written letters of support for the project. Could or should these professionals be considered part of the community? We also had to reflect on whether we should include ourselves in this definition. Although the professionals did not live in the community and were not directly affected by the crimes committed there, they were not entirely outsiders. Some had worked with residents of the area for over 20 years. Could they be considered part of the community? We raised this issue at several meetings with residents and professionals and eventually decided to include the professionals. The definition of community that was emerging, however, told us only a little about the kind of community with which we were dealing. We soon discovered that people living in the housing projects came from a wide range of backgrounds and circumstances. Some were new Canadians. Others were elderly. There were many young families in the buildings, as well as a wide range of ethnic groups. In general, it was a relatively transient population, as people moved in and out fairly regularly. This was not a community based on close, persistent connections, and we had some questions about whether it would be able to support the kind of community-based restorative justice program we envisioned.

We hired staff to assist in establishing the program, although our plan was for them to be short-term employees who would eventually turn the program over to residents. We consulted widely and quickly recognized the need to address issues of diversity and division within the community. We held meetings with representatives of the specific ethnic/cultural groups that made up the largest component of the residents of the housing complexes. We also reached out to young people living in the area. We advertised, organized, and held open public meetings to inform community members of what we were proposing and to invite them to participate. Some participants that self-identified as being interested were trained to lead restorative justice forums.

By taking these steps, we had a de facto definition of community for our project. It emerged in a messy and complicated manner, limited by administrative rules and by our own interests. It involved local residents, but it also included community-based groups and agencies as well as representatives from the municipal housing authority. While our intention was to have the people living in these projects take ownership of the program, the definition of community was essentially imposed by outsiders.

Next, we had to identify which youth we would take into the program. We consulted with the community and got agreement on the criteria to be used. The police, also, agreed to these criteria, and we did a lot of training and consultations with front-line officers to make them aware of the program and what we were trying to accomplish. After almost a year of regular meetings, consultations with different groups, and intensive training for volunteer facilitators, we were ready for our first referral. These developments suggested that the process of responsibilization could actually take place and that it was possible for the state to download responsibility to the community through a program like ours. But was this really the case?

Several factors outside of our control interfered with the intended responsibilization. First, the police departments in the region went through a process of amalgamation just as our project was launched. This resulted in police administrative districts being redefined so that the boundaries we had originally accepted for the project no longer existed. Would this mean we needed to redefine our community? It took considerable time, but eventually we were told that the community we had identified was still acceptable to the police.

Next, we had a challenge getting referrals. Once we had reaffirmed the boundaries of the project, we waited for police referrals so we could begin holding community justice forums. We discovered, however, that the police were not confident that community members could or should facilitate the forums. This was a serious setback. How could we have a community-based restorative justice program if the community could not be involved? In practice, the police felt that criminal justice professionals, not the people living in communities, should run the forums. They had concerns about confidentiality in a small community and were worried that family ties might interfere. In some ways, this was a secondary concern because we received only a few police referrals. However, it was very frustrating to have gone through a year of consultations and negotiations only to have a key partner act this way once the project started.

Even working with our staff as the facilitators, the referrals we did get from the police did not reflect the spirit of the community-based project they had agreed to support. For example, we had several referrals from the police of youth from outside our target community. Rather than viewing our project as a means for returning responsibility for youth justice issues to the local community, the police used it as a way of diverting select youth from the legal system. In one case, the police referred two young people from wealthy families whose parents pressured the authorities to divert them. Even though these youth were not from the target community, the police put pressure on us to take these young people into our program or risk the possibility of losing future referrals. During this stage of the project, the police also referred a suburban youth caught shoplifting and committing vandalism. They wanted this young person dealt with through our project in order to avoid the formal court process and the possibility that this young person might end up with a criminal record.

In our attempt to put a community-based program into practice, we witnessed the emergence of multiple definitions of community. These definitions were influenced by the circumstances, particularly by the power of the police, to determine (initially) who would or could be referred to our program. In many ways, the program became just another type of service provided by professionals who handled cases with no involvement of people living in the community. As we noted above, this type of approach cannot be defined as community-based because it reflects the interests and concerns of the police and other community agencies, not those of the residents of the community.

Given these challenges, we questioned if there was an alternate definition of community we might use. We knew McCold and Wachtel's (1998) thesis that the community is not a place but rather involves the connection between people. They called these connections micro-communities. These are the kind of communities, we argued, where people's strong emotional or personal connections would make participation in a restorative justice project more meaningful for both victims and offenders. Based on this approach, we turned to two other definitions of community—one based on institutional connections (schools) and the other on cultural/symbolic communities of interest.

Schools in the area became the next major source of referrals for the project. School administrators were approached by project staff who described the project and offered to help with incidents involving students. Schools represent an important community for young people, who not only spend a great deal of time there, but who meet and interact with their friends and peers there. School-based forums exemplified many of the elements identified in restorative justice theory. Young people who were involved in incidents at school could make restitution and be reintegrated into the school community in a positive way. The connection students had to their schools and their desire to maintain positive relationships there were the motivation for many of those referred to complete their restorative justice agreements and make amends.

The project staff also met with leaders of local ethnic communities to tell them about the program and ask them to inform their friends and neighbours about it. Community leaders felt the program would benefit their youth and shared the information. They also agreed to participate in the forums and to provide support for the youth involved. This put us into contact with members of the local ethnic community whose children were in conflict with the law. Many sought to participate, and not only were they active in making referrals, they also spoke to defence attorneys about the option. This, eventually, led several defence attorneys to refer youth to the program. The program ran for three years and provided forums for two of the three years. Over 100 youth were assisted. However, once the funding ended, the forums ceased as well.

Several lessons about neoliberalism and the move toward the community can be drawn from this case study. First, defining community in practice is challenging. If the state is committed to a neoliberal approach that downloads responsibility for programs and services to the community, it faces significant challenges in actually identifying communities that are acceptable, willing, and able to do its bidding. Second, while the federal state may be committed to neoliberalism, the impact on state agents, within the criminal justice system and potentially within other state agencies, has to be considered. Are the police willing to give up control of youth diversion? Their resistance can seriously limit the success of neoliberal downloading. Finally, while people are willing to take advantage of opportunities that state funding provides, the lack of sustainability suggests that the state faces enormous challenges in getting the community to row. The state has to consider whether the long-term provision of services and programs by communities is feasible.

Case Study 3.2: Finding Community in a Low-Income Housing Project

Case Study 3.1 considered attempts to define community from the outside in the process of operating a community-based restorative justice project for youth. In this example, we look at how a particular definition of community emerged in a low-income housing complex. This was another project directed at crime prevention; however, in this case, the project was the result of the efforts of a group of residents who wanted to make their community safer for their children. It is an important example of the role of relationships and people's connections to one another in determining how people define community. An important lesson here is how community-based activities can be sustained since sustainable community action is an important consideration for the state in its attempts at responsibilization.

The case study was part of a larger project on the sustainability of community initiatives, which involved in-depth case studies in a number of sites across the country in 2002 and 2003. The community that is the focus of this example was given the code name of Moosehead. A social housing complex consisting of 48 row house units, it was located on the outskirts of a northern community with a population of approximately 9,000. While the housing complex was where the activity took place, the actual definition of community that emerged was more complicated.

Moosehead was located on the periphery of a larger community, and ever since it was developed, it had a bad reputation among people in the town. Being on the edge of town and having poor public transportation further marginalized the residents since they were not a high priority for municipal services and, indeed, had few public resources available to them, not even a park or playground. The several columns of row houses had little space between them. There was no green space for the children to play and no schools within walking distance, so the children were bussed into town.

Moosehead was located within a fixed geographic location with clearly deline-ated boundaries, including a road on one side and a forested area on two others. This contributed to the complex's identification as a distinct community. The housing was publicly owned and subsidized, and many of the people living there were receiving various forms of social assistance and support. These fea-tures—the poverty, the subsidized housing, being on the geographic margins of town—played an important role in the way the residents and others in the town defined the community. The people living in Moosehead were associated with the social problems that were perceived to exist there. But beyond the stigma attached to them, residents of Moosehead were highly isolated from each other. There were no common areas for people to gather or for children to play. There was no community hall or other meeting space, and there was no organized group or association in the complex. By any measure, this was nothing more than a collection of individuals and families who lived in the same place rather than a community, however defined.

Beginning in the 1990s, things began to change. In 1993, there were reports of child sexual abuse, exacerbated by bullying and fights. People grew concerned over the safety of their children, and, on the advice of a local social worker, a few parents got together in one woman's kitchen to discuss what to do. From their shared commitment to protect their children, they identified a number of issues and challenges facing the residents of Moosehead. Slowly, they looked for solutions to these problems. Their first focus was on the need to establish a safe place for children to play. They thought that a good place to start would be to find a way to encourage other parents and children living in the complex to spend more time together doing fun things. In order to do this, however, they needed to connect to the other families in the housing project and with other groups and organizations who could support their efforts.

They took some first steps. With help from a crime prevention group in a nearby city, they organized a family street dance and invited the residents of the housing project, the local RCMP, and some town members interested in crime prevention. The street dance had activities for children and encouraged parents to participate in them with their children. At that time, there were about 300 people living in the housing project, and what was surprising to organizers was that the majority of people took part in the day's activities. It brought people together—they talked about issues and got to know each other. During their discussions, they realized that many residents were concerned about their children having a safe place to play. The question on peoples' minds was what they could do about their common concerns.

The parents who had been at the original meeting approached the provincial housing authority to see if they could establish a place for the children to play. The housing authority helped them do this, and soon a new playground was built. The parents also organized a number of short-term activities throughout the summer, such as a neighbourhood clean-up. More and more people became interested in improving the community. During the winter, they organized friendly contests such as window decorating and held some fundraising activities (mostly within the housing project itself). They also had activities such as story time for small children. They sought donations from local businesses (e.g., grocers and the local garage). In the spring, they resumed activities by holding an Easter egg hunt and family fun days. The organizers made an effort to include young people by having special events for them such as hockey shootouts (with an autographed hockey stick for a prize). They also held activities that engaged parents and children (e.g., hula hoop contests between parents and young people).

As a result of these activities, people living in Moosehead started to take pride in their neighbourhood. For example, young people who had been breaking bottles began to help with the clean-up. The stigma that people living in the community felt from those living in town began to decrease. While people's attitudes about the community were changing, it was and remains an ongoing challenge to shift the attitudes of those outside the housing project about the community and the people who live there. However, those involved in mobilizing the community found that the children and youth responded positively. They were happy to have something constructive to do.

Moosehead has many of the characteristics we commonly associate with the definition of a community, that is, a common place and a common symbolic focus (the safety of their children). As well, those living there have developed an institutional framework to allow them to act collectively. They organized around common concerns, then successfully sought state funding to allow them to achieve their goals. In many ways, this is the community envisioned by the neoliberal state—it requires limited government involvement and uses government funds to achieve outcomes that are in line with state priorities. Further, the activity has persisted for over a decade and a half.

Do these things make Moosehead a community? Is this the kind of community that is envisioned by the neoliberal state? If it is, there are key challenges that need to be addressed by the state because this community emerged around a local agenda that was meaningful to those involved. Whether it can be engaged by the neoliberal state to achieve its own agenda, however, is questionable. The community has been willing to come together and act on issues that it has identified. Will it be willing to do the bidding of others, specifically representatives of the state? This is an open question, and one that must be addressed on a case by case basis.

Case Study 3.3: Community on Its Face—Fragmentation Sub Rosa

The third case study presents an example of how a particular community dealt with neoliberal state funding. The questions remain the same: how is community defined, and can such communities be engaged as effective agents of state policy?

Marionville (a pseudonym) is a large town with a high concentration of wealthy middle- and upper-middle-class suburban neighbourhoods. It is dominated by single-family homes where both parents work and where children and youth are enrolled in music lessons, sports, and other recreational activities. The local high school is well attended, and most students graduate. Crime is low, although there is some concern about bush parties and some problems with occasional vandalism and break-ins. Overall, however, on the surface Marionville appears to be the model of a successful, prosperous, and pleasant community.

Our research in Marionville was part of the larger study of the sustainability of community safety initiatives. We focused on a youth-led appeal to the Rotary Club for funding for a camp designed to train youth for a leadership role within the schools and the wider community. The issues raised by the youth in their successful funding presentation caused a number of the adults to reflect on what they had been told about the concerns of young people in the community.

Several of the Rotary Club members had been exposed to materials on community asset building developed by the Search Institute, which identified 40 developmental assets described as "positive experiences and personal qualities that young people need to grow up healthy, caring, and responsible" (Search Institute 2002). This approach is part of the neoliberal move to community and seeks to identify what communities need to do to meet the challenges of taking responsibility for the success of their community and their people.

The Rotary Club members thought that knowing the level of assets in the community and any potential gaps might be useful in addressing the concerns that the youth had identified in their presentation. They consulted with a number of active community members, and it was agreed that they would call a community-wide meeting to present the plan to do an assets survey. At that meeting they made a case for action, and a plan was developed to implement the survey. This led to the establishment of the Assets Development Initiative (ADI). A survey of youth in the community was conducted. While the group leading the initiative thought that there might be small gaps in the assets available to youth in the community, the survey revealed that the community was weak on 18 of the 40 developmental assets when compared to other communities in the large Search Institute database. Specifically, the survey showed that youth felt isolated, devalued, and lacked intergenerational contacts. In addition, they did not feel safe in their schools and felt unwelcome in the wider community.

The survey findings exposed the divisions within what the adults had assumed was a strong and healthy community. They believed that because the youth were "their" children and because the adults viewed the community as a positive space, their children would automatically feel like members and be welcome and included.

Here, again, the case study shows that people on the ground who identify community as a geographical place believe that living within the municipal boundaries by itself guarantees membership. In practice, the youth presentation and the assets survey revealed that young people were not as valued as adults thought and that they felt excluded and pushed to the margins. For instance, at a focus group we conducted, young people told us that the store across the street from the high school had a sign directing that only two teenagers were allowed in the store at a time. This practice was instituted to curb shoplifting and theft. The message the students received was that because someone had stolen from the store, all young people were seen as potential criminals and were treated that way. They were watched when they entered and followed around as they shopped. Only when one student left was another let in.

The results of the assets survey were widely shared and served as the basis for a community-wide mobilization. A range of groups and organizations got involved. The municipality covered the cost of hiring a part-time coordinator and provided office space in City Hall. The coordinator worked to garner the support of city residents and local voluntary groups. The ADI generated a number of programs intended to build assets in the community, including establishing a speakers club for youth, leadership classes within the high school, a greeters program that brought seniors into the schools, and a breakfast club. As the asset building continued, the need for more recreational opportunities in the community led to the establishment of a Boys and Girls Club. A building was donated by the city and was renovated with donated materials and volunteer labour. As energy was directed at establishing the club, the ADI moved into the background. The Boys and Girls Club assumed responsibility for the activities the ADI previously oversaw.

Activities related to building assets for youth continued. The coordinator applied for funding to develop programming for youth using a "crime prevention through social development (CSPD)" model. The initiative involved the business community and the Chamber of Commerce and focused on building entrepreneurial skills with high-risk youth—a sub-group of youth identified as being even more marginal than others. The new program operates two retail outlets to teach young people various retail skills such as pricing, advertising, purchasing, marketing, and customer service. It brings together instructional and hands-on components, and it generates funds to support other youth initiatives in the community, including the Boys and Girls Club.

Here, an entire municipality took responsibility for and mobilized to meet the needs of its children and youth. Many individuals, groups, and organizations were involved. Youth were given opportunities for input. The premise was that the local community was responsible for its youth. The community was identified as a geographic location, a very large area encompassing very different kinds of places. It shares with the previous example a commitment and concern for youth—though framed as the lack of assets to make the community a positive and vibrant place for youth.

There is some symbolic connection here as well, since there is a belief in community building as the way to ensure a strong community. There is also an acceptance of local rather than state responsibility for meeting community needs. The case study has some important implications for the state as it seeks to find communities to take on the responsibility for what were previously state programs and services. The initiative in Marionville has been sustained and has been able to generate funds locally to support its activities. It seems to fit the neoliberal responsibilized community almost perfectly and suggests that there is a possibility of successfully downloading responsibility to the local level. The question is, how can these factors be incorporated more broadly by the neoliberal state?

To ascertain whether other communities can be responsibilized, the state must determine which features are required to help make the move to the community successful. In the case of Marionville, a stable middle-class community, including a business community willing to get involved, mobilized a variety of resources. This suggests an acceptance of neoliberal philosophy in as much as people in the community thought that the young people should be taught how to be responsible for themselves. Getting and holding a job are important indicators of individual responsibility. However, the capacity in Marionville is not typical of most communities. It has a large number of capable individuals who are willing and able to work on behalf of the community. Many communities struggle with issues of capacity, and most have not been able to do what Marionville did.

The Neoliberal Community?

The case studies presented in this chapter demonstrate the challenges related to defining and identifying a community on the ground. They show many of the potential difficulties that await the neoliberal state as it engages in the move toward the community and the process of responsibilization. The first challenge is how to define community. In the past, policy was enacted by the state and began with a definition of community that was place-based. The focus was on finding an administrative site for the delivery of programs and services. This type of thinking was reflected in the first example in which the state developed a program that identified key actors to work on behalf of the community. It showed that, in practice, community-based initiatives do not work well with such definitions. The use of geographic, administrative definitions in the restorative justice project quickly fell apart. Perhaps the greatest challenge was related to the resistance by criminal justice professionals to share some of their jurisdictional power.

This initiative also showed the range of potential definitions of community that can emerge or be identified in the process of working at the community level. The connections between people are often more important than place-based notions of community. Our experience with restorative justice forums in schools and in ethnic communities showed that they are places that connect people. However, the lack of community ownership of the project had an important impact since the forums did not persist once the funding ended. As we saw in the two other case studies, sustainability of community-based activity requires the community to take ownership of both problems and their solutions. When local ownership and buy-in does not occur, the state is unlikely to be able to successfully enact sustainable initiatives.

Another issue is the possible tension between the state's ability to direct the activities in which responsibilized communities engage and sustainability. In the second case study, a strong sense of community emerged as people came together to meet common goals. While they accepted state funding, this was directed by them to their own concerns. To the extent that their concerns matched those of the state, they would accept responsibility. It is not clear, however, whether this community had the willingness or capacity to do much more, that is, become more active agents of the state.

Finally, we need to consider the question of not just capacity but also the issues being addressed. In the third case study, there was a lot of capacity; people mobilized around a common concern and sought to responsibilize youth, a notion that fits well within the ideology of both neoliberalism and the local business community. How well would this community respond to other social issues, especially those that are more controversial? Would they have been willing to launch as vigorous a campaign in response to a community survey on racism or domestic violence? While most people agree that investing in youth is a good thing, there is much denial of systemic racism, and domestic violence is considered by many to be a private issue. The question remains whether the state will be able to download responsibility for more controversial issues to the community.

Chapter 4

CAN THE NEOLIBERAL STATE SET THE AGENDA? THE CHALLENGES OF POWER AND POLITICS

Introduction

An important aspect to the rise of neoliberalism and the move toward the community is the attempt by the state to control the local agenda by exercising its power through strategies such as responsibilization. The state, however, is not the only actor with the power to influence the local agenda. There are numerous groups and organizations working at the community level, each with its own goals and mandates, and each willing and able to exercise power to achieve its own ends. What are the implications of this for the state? Once again, trying to understand what happens on the ground in communities is neither simple nor straightforward. The policies and practices of the neoliberal state have been introduced into an existing context that features remnants of the previous regime as well as a web of existing power relations that temper what the state is able to do. While the state tries to use its power to control the local agenda, it must also take into account other powerful actors on the scene—including the public.

The case studies presented in this chapter demonstrate how the consequences of the state's use of power in downloading responsibility onto communities, and the process of responsibilization more generally, are complex and often contradictory. Specifically, the case studies look at how the neoliberal state has tried to use its funding to control the local agenda in communities across the country by identifying with whom it will work and prioritizing the issues, programs, and services it wants to fund. However, as we have seen in previous chapters, the state's power to control funding is no guarantee that its policies or programs will be either implemented as planned or supported by the community.

Importantly, the state has tried to legitimize its use of power in the move toward the community through an appeal to an active citizenry and the opportunity this provides for more local democracy. This strategy, however, has received mixed reviews. On the one hand, the state's engagement of the community in program and service delivery has been hailed by those who see the move toward the community as a positive development well-suited to the challenges of modern society. They view this as a way of rekindling civic engagement (Putnam 1995) and restoring the public's faith in the political and institutional order (Brooks and Cheng 2001; Rose and Pettersen 2000). Fontan et al. (2009) found new forms of collaboration emerged to open up new possibilities in Montreal communities. Similarly, while examining communities in Latin America, Jackiewicz (2006) demonstrated that the shift toward the community has allowed some communities to exercise more local control over effective development.

For more critical commentators, however, the move toward the community signals the emergence of a fundamental shift in power as external agencies gain increasing control over and in communities (Cheshire and Lawrence 2005; Cohen 1985; Crawford 1998, 1999; DeFilippis et al. 2006; Garland 2001; Geddes 2006; Graddy and Morgan 2006; Hartman 2005; Levi 2008; Pavlich 1996). Some argue that the emergence of community-based responses to what had previously been social concerns (e.g., community safety, mental health, health care, housing, poverty) has increasingly allowed the state to set the agenda for local actors (municipal governments, non-governmental organizations, and individual citizens) by making them increasingly responsible for these areas. In the process, the state has relieved itself of the responsibility for continuing to provide key programs and services while maintaining its control at a distance. Thus, while the state acknowledges the need to address issues, it attempts to shift the responsiblity for meeting them onto other actors. This includes making individuals more responsible (e.g., for their own health and safety) and the emergence of a plethora of groups and agencies working in communities on a wide range of social issues.

At the community level, there are a number of players besides the state that actively exercise power. The exercising of power is often visible in the relationships that different actors in the community have with one another. Sometimes these are supportive and collegial, and sometimes they are conflictual. For example, there is often intense competition over limited financial, human, physical, and symbolic resources. Several contemporary critics have raised concerns over the potentially negative consequences that may occur as a result of competing or conflicting power groups operating at the community level (Cohen 1985; Garland 2001; Graddy and Morgan 2006; O'Malley 1992; Pavlich 1996; Rose 1996). Concerns have been raised about the development of local oligarchies that deploy undemocratic, unrepresentative networks of special interests. In some cases, these oligarchies can marginalize various groups in a community, especially those in the at-risk categories (Pavlich 1996; Crawford 1999). The diverse power nodes that exist at the local level have meant that the move toward the community is not easy or automatic.

DeFillipis et al. (2006) caution that we must neither over-romanticize nor over-vilify the move toward the community. On the positive side, Graddy and Morgan's (2006) work on the role of philanthropic foundations shows that increasingly these organizations are able to fill the void left by state budget cutbacks and assist communities to meet local needs. But they also caution that success is shaped by the features of both the community and the supporting organizations.

The case studies in Chapter 3 showed that there are a variety of groups who potentially can play a leadership role in a community, and this is often related to who holds power there. The critical question is which groups and organizations are recognized as representing community-based interests. Stenson and Watt (1999) argue that only certain groups are acknowledged by the state as governmental; that is, only certain groups are recognized by the state as being appropriate partners in delivering the state's agenda through community-based programs. These groups include philanthropic, religious, educational, professional, political party and/or media-oriented social movements, and commercial organizations. These often compete with other groups and organizations whose agendas, networks, and working practices are unacceptable to the state. The groups that are allowed entrée into what they term the web of control can have a direct impact on what goes on in practice at the local level since they will have the resources to act. Moreover, they can play an important role in excluding particular individuals or groups from participating in decision-making or service delivery. They can also decide what strategies will be deemed acceptable and what potential solutions to community problems will receive consideration.

The ability of the state to exercise power faces a number of challenges. There are two key mechanisms that it uses to determine activity at the communitiy level. The first is through control over funding for programs and services. To receive funding a group or organization must address state-identified issues and meet state funding critiera. Second is requiring those receiving state funds to work in partnership with others in the community. This seems to be a benign requirement since, in most cases, effective action to address issues within a community requires a number of players to cooperate and even share responsibility. For example, the outbreak of an infectious disease may require a wide range of public health agencies to work with schools, senior's centres, and other community institutions to ensure that it is kept in check. Community-wide cooperation is also visible in various public safety campaigns and fundraising events. Given this, the state's expectation that people work together is not surprising. However, requiring otherwise independent agencies to do so can result in some unintended and negative outcomes. In some cases, agencies that are recognized by the state as acceptable partners may be unwilling to work with others because they fear the competition or want to protect their own TURF. In other cases, agencies may be willing to work together but are prohibited from doing so as a result of boundary restrictions, agency rules, or laws precluding information sharing, especially about clients. So, the state must contend both with resistance to partnerships and the challenges of making them work effectively.

Partnerships and Project Funding

As noted above, the neoliberal state requires community groups and organizations to work with partners as a condition of receiving state funding. While the overt purpose of requiring partnerships is that they are a way of ensuring that a proposed project addresses an issue of significant concern in a community, they have become a way for the state to exercise its power to set the local agenda. Partnerships have expanded exponentially under neoliberalism.

Crawford (1998), for example, argues that the expansion of partnerships within the area of crime prevention has been a quiet revolution. There have been increasing efforts by the state to connect the traditional means of responding to crime (law enforcement) with multi-sector approaches to policy development and service delivery. The objective of these efforts is to promote the responsibilization of the community by fostering a broader role for it in crime prevention and control. According to Crawford, partnerships along with community and prevention form the new trilogy of many governmental efforts to address crime. Yet little is known about the concept of partnership or the processes of partnership that can lead to successful outcomes.

In its most commonsense form, partnership is understood as a way of working together. It is seen to be effective because of its appeal as a holistic, problem-focused approach; its potential to foster a grassroots rather than a top-down strategy for solving problems; and the possibility it will produce results that cannot be achieved in isolation.

When placed under closer scrutiny, however, a common definition of partnership is elusive. This is because working together means many different things to different people. In practice, partnership encapsulates many types of relationships and approaches. The nature of the roles, the degree of formality, and the LINKAGES (HORIZONTAL AND/OR VERTICAL) vary considerably. Some partnerships may be long-term with extensive connections, formal ties, and horizontal linkages. Others may be short-term, informal, and vertically linked. This diversity poses a number of challenges, especially if partners have different expectations about their respective roles and responsibilities. An important axiom related to success is that mutual understanding is necessary if partnerships are to be mutually satisfactory.

BOX 4.1: A PARTNERSHIP TYPOLOGY

| Consultative | Cooperative | Coordinated | Collaborative |

Partnerships have been an important requirement of state funding programs under Canadian neoliberalism. Groups and agencies do form partnerships, but these vary considerably in the degree to which they involve the features of full partnership—working together to deliver a program with shared responsibility for program financing, delivery, and outcomes. There are four main types of partnership, which represent a continuum from consultative partnerships at one end of the scale to collaborative partnerships at the other. In the move from one end of this continuum to the other, the roles, responsibilities, and expectations for participants change. In consultative partnerships, the working relationship between partners is limited, extending only to keeping each other informed of plans and activities. The interaction is limited, and partner expectations are low. In collaborative partnerships, expectations can be quite high. Collaborative partnerships can involve joint decision-making and shared responsibility for action and budgets. While there is no ideal type of partnership, the form chosen should be well understood by all parties with roles and responsibilities clearly laid out. Failure to do so can lead to serious problems, including disappointment over unmet expectations, a breakdown in communication, and the eventual dissolution of the partnership.

(Canada 2002)

On the one hand, it could be argued that it may not be realistic, or even desirable, to try to overly confine the concept of partnership, as elasticity allows it to be organic and evolving. On the other, the lack of definition—and, hence, parameters to the relationship—is not without risk. Different perceptions of the rationale, principles, and values behind the partnership, and how it will work in practice, may contribute to stressful operational environments and may limit its effectiveness.

The effectiveness of partnerships can be challenged by a variety of factors. A great deal depends on how the partnership is structured and the processes used to implement it. Reaching agreement and implementing partnership arrangements can be particularly complex when there are many sectors or agencies involved. Power relations, operational dynamics, and protecting turf are all potentially troublesome if there are no mechanisms established to manage expectations or resolve problems. Lack of communication and lack of clarity about issues that are important to partners (e.g., constraints of confidentiality); failure to be inclusive (especially of those who work with clients); questions of trust (a fundamental dynamic in inter-agency relations); and the reality of competition, conflict, and organizational autonomy are all potential stresses on partnerships.

State Power and the Local

Partnerships are a key aspect of neoliberalism, at least in the Canadian context. As the case studies will show, developing working partnerships at the community level is a challenge. When key groups and agencies choose not to work together, a project can end quickly once funding runs out. Thus, while there is the illusion of building partnerships in the process of accessing state funding, these are not necessarily effective working relationships. On the other hand, when partnerships are viewed as positive, they can help community-based initiatives to flourish. The state can require partnerships, and groups and agencies can engage in building connections to receive funding, but the state cannot ensure that effective partnerships will develop.

In this section, we consider three case studies that highlight examples of the relationship between highly successful community-based initiatives and the exercise of power by the state through its control over funding. Each example helps to illustrate the limits of state power, including its ability to set the local agenda through control over funding. The first two case studies are part of a larger research project on sustainable community initiatives while the third is from a project undertaken by one of the authors in conjunction with the Federation of Canadian Municipalities (FCM, a representative agency of municipal governments across the country). All three studies used a similar methodology: in-depth interviews and focus group sessions with key informants from a wide variety of sectors including social services, law enforcement, education, health, and municipal government. In Case Study 4.1, the state provided funding for community activities, but who set the agenda became an issue. In Case Study 4.2, the state offered to provide funds to an existing and highly successful community group that was already working to meet needs that had been identified by community members themselves. In the end, this group decided to turn down the state's offer of funding. Case Study 4.3 considers an initiative that involved a federal government department working with the FCM who, in turn, sought to engage local communities in developing a strategy to address drug issues. The policy initiative was supported by the federal government in response to a need identified by municipal leaders with FCM acting as a broker to engage local communities.

Case Study 4.1: State Funding within a Local Initiative
The first case study revisits Marionville, the middle-/upper-middle-class suburban community discussed in Case Study 3.3 (see pp. 61–63). The community was dismayed with the results of a review of the developmental assets available to its youth. Community leaders were particularly disturbed to discover that their young people felt marginalized and unwelcome. The municipal government was involved in funding the assets building portion of the initiative, but they

eventually turned the program over to the Boys and Girls Club. At this point, the funding that the municipality had been providing for a project coordinator ended. In response, the coordinator looked for other sources of funding to address ongoing and unmet needs related to high-risk youth.

The coordinator was eventually able to secure funds from the National Crime Prevention Centre's Business Action Program, while local Chamber of Commerce members focused on a project to build the entrepreneurial skills of high-risk youth by operating two retail outlets. The smaller of the two was a thrift shop that depended on donations from people in the community. The youth participating in the program did minor repairs and refurbished donated goods to prepare them for sale. It was a break-even enterprise. The second outlet sold end-of-line or overstocked items purchased in bulk from a large retail corporation. This merchandise proved to appeal to local consumers, resulting in a healthy profit for the store. Part of the profit was used to pay the young workers according to their effort and performance. Some was used to buy more stock and expand what was available. The rest was used to support youth activities in the community, including the activities at the Boys and Girls Club and keeping the less profitable thrift shop going.

The funding provided through the federal government's Business Action Program helped to get the project started, but the initiative eventually generated its own funds. Ensuring the resources necessary to continue to work within the community after initial state funding is a critical concern both for communities and for the state. This community found a way to generate its own funds, thus making it independent of the municipal and federal governments and marking it as a successful neoliberal responsibilized community. Responsibility for the ongoing success of the project required a mechanism (here an umbrella committee) for ensuring that new projects are initiated and ongoing projects continue to receive information and feedback. The municipal government shifted responsibility for management of the initiative to the Boys and Girls Club.

In this community, federal funding was used to further a locally identified need. Did this mean that the central state set the agenda? It did have an impact on what the community was eventually able to do, but it did not set the agenda. Rather, the process of agenda setting occurred prior to funds being provided by the federal government. Local concerns over high-risk youth matched those of the federal government, so the community was able to act on its interests and gain funding. It is not clear what would have happened if these funds had not been available. The entrepreneurial spirit of community members, however, suggests that they would have found other ways to pursue their own interests.

Another important point to note from this case study is that the project undertaken by the community was sustained once the federal funding stopped. The community had developed a market mechanism to meet its needs. This meant that the influence of the state on local decisions and activities was negligible.

The state had no mechanisms for influencing the issues that the community chose to address. The self-sustaining nature of the project allowed community decision-makers to set the local agenda, define issues and needs, and develop strategies to address them.

Case Study 4.2: Refusing State Funding

The second case study, also part of the larger project on sustainable crime prevention in Canada, concerned the development and operation of the Resiliency Centre by the John Howard Society of Saint John, New Brunswick. Saint John is a port city that serves as the regional centre for the surrounding area. The John Howard Society (JHS), a group whose mandate is working with adult male offenders and their families, is the sponsoring agency for the project. This agency has one of the highest caseloads in the province with an average of 3,400 people being released into the community from correctional institutions each year. The Resiliency Centre was started in order to provide an organizational home for a grassroots initiative that developed in the community and that is operated by community volunteers.

The initiative began as the JHS reflected on its role in the community and looked toward the future. It invited a group of community members, leaders of key community organizations, retired professionals, and other service providers with whom it worked to participate in a discussion about their community and its service needs. The needs of children and youth in the community were identified as a high priority which placed the director in an awkward position because the identified needs did not match the mandate of the JHS. However, after gaining a commitment from others in the community to do its part, he agreed to lend his agency's support to the project.

Another challenge was how to have a new initiative with no new funds. The director of the JHS made an interesting proposal. He suggested that each person should consider what they were willing to contribute, and in this spirit he asked his own staff whether the priorities identified at the community meeting were sufficiently important to them to convince them to devote some of their own volunteer time to the initiative. The director explained this strategy by stating that he would not ask others to do things that he himself was not prepared to do. He enlisted the support of 20 people who were willing and able to volunteer their time. An additional 20 volunteers were recruited from the community, including representatives from other social service agencies and community members.

In order to keep the activities of the community initiative separate and distinct from the ongoing activities of the JHS, its Board of Directors suggested that a new organization be established. With this in mind, the Resiliency Centre was created with a mandate to develop and deliver programs for children and youth and their families in the community.

Once established, the Centre received requests from community groups for specific programs. For example, bullying was identified as a serious concern in a local school. The Centre offered to work with the school group to clearly define the need and to develop an appropriate response. Those directly involved were required to provide some basic resources, including a place to meet and volunteers to help run the program. Centre staff then worked with the local community members to develop an appropriate program. They quickly developed a strategy for addressing locally identified problems: if an existing program was available, Centre staff determined what it would cost to acquire it and then they would seek the necessary funding from local sources. If no existing program met the specific need, a local professional social worker would be hired to develop a tailored program.

Local service clubs and businesses are approached with funding requests to cover the costs of buying or developing program materials. This typically involves a request for a few thousand dollars. The Centre approaches supporters on a rotating basis so as not to overtax them. As well, once a Centre staff member is trained, he or she provides training to other community members and agency representatives. Those service providers who have training budgets and who can afford to pay for staff training do so and, in this way, also add to the Centre's funds. Training raises the level of HUMAN CAPITAL available in the community and results in a pool of trained and available community volunteers.

By using volunteer labour—both lay and professional—and space provided by local communities, the Centre has managed to deliver programs for minimal costs. It has run successfully this way since 1995 and continues to operate as an autonomous and independent community resource. It has expanded its programming exponentially and now offers a wide range of programs and services to several thousand youth and families each year. Moreover, news of its success has spread to many neighbouring communities who have approached the Centre and asked for its assistance in establishing their own grassroots initiatives based on its model.

The activities provided by the Centre respond directly to needs identified by the community or specific requests for programs by community groups or agencies such as schools. All Centre programs are developed in response to an identified need and are premised on the fact that members of the community feel strongly enough about the program to provide the physical and human resources required to offer it. These programs could not operate without community support. There are no fixed programs, and programs are added or dropped as community needs are identified or change.

The little funding that is needed is used to support established programs, purchase program materials (booklets, etc.), or send staff for training. As such, the financial requirements are only a fraction of the value added by the Centre to the community. A long list of community, provincial, and federal funding sources has been developed by the Centre over time. Since it only seeks support from a funding agency every second year, most are willing to help if they can. The Centre's requests for funding are also viewed favourably by potential funders who can see that the community is contributing its share. Potential funders are not asked to pay for meeting spaces or staff salaries. This contributes immensely to the ability of the Centre to raise funds since it can show its supporters how their funds are being used to meet a community need. Finally, the Centre can demonstrate that after initial start-up funding, financial requirements for continuing to run the program are minimal. This is important since it is much easier to ask organizations for small amounts of funding on an ongoing basis.

One of the most appealing features of the Centre is that money goes to the people in need of support and services—none of its funding goes to staff, buildings, or administration. Each dollar is used to assist people in the community. To get a sense of the cost savings that the Centre's model allows, it assessed how much it would cost to deliver its programs with paid staff instead of volunteers. With paid staff and with a dedicated budget for office space, a conservative estimate came to $111,369 per year. The actual cost of offering its programs and services to hundreds of local children and youth and their families was $4,613 per year (Caputo et al. 2004). In the words of one volunteer, this economic use of resources has been "a real selling point" (personal communication) for the Centre.

Those responsible for running the Centre have had ongoing discussions about the implications of taking funding from external sources and especially from different levels of government. As they see it, external funding agencies often want to set the needs agenda. This is a serious concern for the Centre since it is dedicated to meeting local needs as defined by local community members and financial support from government agencies comes with strings attached. For their part, government agencies have been slow to change the way they operate with respect to responding to local needs. The terms and conditions under which most of them operate require them to maintain control over how their funds are used and, indirectly, how needs are identified and met. The success enjoyed by the Centre in meeting important community needs has meant that many government agencies have offered funding. Perhaps this is not surprising since this would allow the funders to share in the success enjoyed by the Centre. On the other hand, the Centre has refused to relinquish its control over what programs it offers and whom it serves. It retains the power to set its own agenda and to respond to the needs identified by members of its community.

The Resiliency Centre is another example of how a community can organize to meet its own needs. Is this neoliberalism at work? The short answer is no because the needs the Centre meets were never the responsibility of the state. The Centre did not result from downloading. However, the question of responsibilization is somewhat less clear. Is it a case of people being made responsible for services?

No, quite the contrary. In this community, people wanted to take responsiblity for issues of local concern, and they rejected the state's attempt to have a role and to influence the local agenda. This is grassroots democracry at work.

Case Study 4.3: A State-led Initiative

The third case study was part of the Model Municipal Drug Strategy project, which was undertaken by the FCM from 2000 to 2003. Phase I of this project involved the preparation of materials to assist communities in developing local drug strategies. In Phase II, nine communities used these materials to develop local strategies tailored to meet specific community concerns related to drug use. Phase III assessed their experiences, including the factors that contributed to their success as well as the barriers they encountered. Phase II pilot project communities were provided limited funds ($13,500 each) and one year to put their local drug strategy in place. This case study highlights what happened in one of the pilot project communities, here named Centre Town.

This initiative was a combined effort involving FCM and the National Crime Prevention Centre (NCPC). FCM took the lead in running the project, and its first step was to invite member municipalities to participate. The Centre Town city council agreed to participate and established a committee with 15 members, each agreeing to serve a one-year term. They invited local stakeholders to a meeting and followed that with a letter asking for their feedback. In all, the committee approached 60 to 70 regional agencies involved in addictions issues and drugs in particular. It developed a policy statement that was supported by the municipal government. The municipality also agreed to provide additional funding beyond that provided by FCM in the first year as well as support to take them through the following year. The vision of the municipality was to involve the broader region in the model drug strategy project since Centre Town is a regional centre that provides services to the surrounding area. To this end, the committee sought to partner with groups from outside the city as well as those from within.

The Centre Town committee set a number of goals. It sought to raise awareness of the drug issue in the community, a particularly challenging effort since many in the community denied there was a drug problem despite evidence to the contrary. The committee also faced the challenge of getting the community to take some ownership of the problem and not leave it up to the police and a few service providers to deal with the issue.

The success of the Model Municipal Drug Strategy in Centre Town was mixed. There were some activities that the committee could undertake because of its link to city council. For example, it could develop the model drug policy statement and work to get the city council to support it. It was also able to develop a policy to address awareness through by-laws on grow-ops (buildings used as grow operations for marijuana). It had some influence on supporting the control of drug use and sales in the community through promoting increased law enforcement. It prepared and distributed a resources inventory that identified all the groups and agencies in the community providing programs and services related to drug use. Finally, it was successful in raising awareness of the initiative itself as its work became recognized among stakeholders and community members alike. However, the committee found it challenging to engage the groups it contacted. What proved even more difficult was getting these community groups to develop a coordinated approach and to develop working partnerships.

While the committee was able to gain the support of some community members and agencies eventually and even to develop some partnerships, it found that focusing attention on substance abuse was tough, especially when controversial issues emerged during discussions about how to respond to these concerns (e.g., the role of harm reduction strategies versus treatment versus law enforcement). In many respects, the committee found it difficult to get people to leave their own agendas at the door and to join it in its work. It was even more challenging, despite tremendous effort, to get youth involved. There was also conflict and resistance from various agencies, especially those who had been working in the area before the committee started its initiative. This was their turf, and they had their own sense of the issues and what responses were needed. Thus, the initiative in Centre Town did not persist once the funding for the program ended. This was the case even though there was considerable agreement that it addressed a significant concern in the community.

Why did this initiative fail? Clearly it came from outside the community. It attempted to focus some community attention on drug-related issues. However, the committee met with a variety of challenges as it tried to get groups and individuals to participate. Municipal and federal resources were used to set the agenda at the local level and to force the community to address a particular problem—drug use. And while the local city council invested time, resources, and money in trying to mobilize the community to take action, the attempt to set the local agenda did not work. To some extent, the initiative failed because community members were unwilling to acknowledge that drugs were a problem in their community. Resistance also was due to the fact that there were existing groups and organizations that had a vested interest in the issue and that were pursuing their own agendas. Thus, the intentions of both the federal and municipal governments to set the agenda were unsuccessful, and the attempt to develop a sustainable community-based response failed.

Using state power over funding to influence the local agenda presents challenges. As the case studies above illustrate, success is more likely when issues are of local importance and when groups and agencies access government funds because they resonate with local concerns. Success is less likely when direction is externally established without consideration for local conditions or for the concerns of the community. Programs or services have to be meaningful to those invoved if they are to be accepted and supported. When the state is merely a source of temporary funding that requires certain types of activities, the programs do not persist. However, in taking funds from the state, there is a recognition that the state will seek to set the agenda for what is needed, important, or required. Those accepting state funding know that there are strings attached and respond accordingly.

Agreeing to Work Together

In this section, some of the challenges faced by communities as they attempt to meet state funding criteria related to working in partnerships are examined. Some were successful in meeting state program funding criteria, and some were not.

Case Study 4.4: Resistance to Collaboration

This case study looks again at the restorative justice project described in Case Study 3.1, but this time focusing on the partnership with the police. The initiative began with a decision to put forward a funding application for a federal program by a youth-serving agency in collaboration with researchers at a local university. Before submitting the application, the agency invited residents and representatives of other agencies working in the target communities to a meeting to discuss the possibilities of working together on a project of mutual interest. It contacted a wide array of stakeholders—the police, the Crown attorney's office, local health and social services agencies, the housing authority, and the tenants' associations in the two communities identified as potential sites for the project. These groups were provided with information about the proposal and asked for their input and suggestions as well as their willingness to participate in the project as a partner. Letters in support of the project were provided by over 40 groups, agencies, and individuals, including the police and the Crown attorney's office who were deemed to be essential to the project as they would be the sources of referrals.

In addition to letters of support, specific and in-depth consultations were held with the police and the Crown attorney's office with respect to protocols and procedures for dealing with referrals, the types of referrals, and the criteria to be used to determine whether a case was suitable for the project. Detailed strategies were developed with these agencies to ensure that once the project started, it would run smoothly and to the benefit of the young people and the community while meeting the legal requirements of pertinent legislation as well as other regulations governing the operations of these two criminal justice agencies. Officers from the store-front police station in one of the communities were contacted personally and given detailed information about the project. They were advised of the letters of support signed by their agency as well as the extensive planning that had taken place regarding the operation of the program.

Once funding was in place, staff were hired and trained, and office space was secured and furnished. At this point, the project was ready to receive referrals. Changes in youth justice legislation (the Youth Criminal Justice Act) had made diversion programs a priority. The legislation also required the police to justify not diverting youth. In light of these changes and based on the youth crime statistics provided by the police for the project communities, the project anticipated receiving about 100 referrals per year.

Once all this had been done, the agency waited for referrals, but none came. Over and over the police were asked for an explanation for this lack of referrals. Police and Crown contacts reiterated everything was in order and that officers in the district would be reminded about the program and its objectives. Still no referrals came from the police in the project communities. Instead, a trickle of referrals came from police officers outside of the target area. These cases primarily involved middle- or upper-middle-class Caucasian youth. None met the criteria that had been established in conjunction with the police when the project was designed. When the project staff refused to hear the first case, the police called them repeatedly; the officer in charge went to the funding agency director and pressured him to have the project take the case. This suggests that when the police perceived referrals to be either in their interest or perhaps when they viewed the offenders as deserving, the chances of them making a referral to the program increased. When this was not the case, young people were simply processed through the formal justice system. The Crown was similarly unwilling to refer cases; over three years only three referrals were received despite ongoing Crown promises to divert youth to the program.

The program required the police to exercise their discretion in order to refer youth, but doing so meant more than simply diverting these young people from the formal justice system (in this case the courts). Deciding to refer a young person to the program meant that the police were giving up the right to determine what would happen. This challenged traditional definitions of both policing and of justice—making a referral to the program required the police to forego much of their authority for responding to youth and, in effect, to relinquish some of their power. What does this say about the state's requirement that those applying for funding work in partnership? In this example, two key partners were the police and the Crown attorney, both of them state agencies that might be expected to go along with the funding priorities of the national state. However, their own funding was not dependent on cooperating in local partnerships, and there was little to compel them to act in good faith. Letters of support and good public relations aside, neither the police nor the Crown attorney had much to gain by collaborating with a community-based program, but both apparently felt they had something to lose—their power and control over the criminal justice process in their jurisdiction. The promise of working in a productive partnership obviously did not overcome the potential loss of power such a partnership would entail.

Case Study 4.5: Successful Collaboration—Working Together Despite the Rules

We discovered a completely different process underway while doing research in a large public housing project in western Canada in 2003–04. This community consisted of a high-density neighbourhood in a large urban centre. Residents included many lower-income families living in 400 social housing units and 10 low-rise rental apartment complexes in close proximity to one another. There were also some modest single-family homes on the periphery of this neighbourhood. Altogether, there were approximately 1,200 children—mainly from lower-income, single-parent households—living within a six-block radius. Several years ago, this community was identified as "high risk" based on the number of calls for service received by the local police. When the local initiative began, the police reported that the crime rate was the seventh highest of 32 neighbourhoods in the city.

The core of the initiative was the development of a working relationship—a partnership—among community residents and those providing services. What developed was a way for people to change the way things had been done in the past. They were able to come up with strategies for doing business that made more sense for both those living in the community as well as those working there. Essentially, the initiative required that barriers be broken down between service providers and their professional organizations, as well as those between service providers and community members.

The community coalition that developed served as a vehicle through which service providers and community residents could come together to identify needs and mobilize the resources needed to meet them. It has led to greater cooperation among service providers and has included efforts to make services more accessible to community residents who in the past were often unwilling and/or unable to access them. In doing this, the service providers involved in the coalition focused on achieving community development objectives, including some that were often outside the mandate of the organizations for which they worked. In many cases, these workers struggled to make things happen in the community in spite of, rather than with the support of, the agencies that employed them.

This initiative began when several neighbourhood service providers (the police, the school, and a community social worker) came together to discuss their concerns. It soon became apparent that they shared a commitment to the community. This was the common ground on which they formed a partnership group, which eventually led to the establishment of the community coalition. Its members focused on projects that encouraged service providers and community members to work together to make the community a safer and healthier place. Specific activities were undertaken as needs or issues were identified by the coalition such as providing more recreational opportunities for youth or cleaning up the local park. They tried to show the residents that they were serious about making positive changes and worked hard to achieve some immediate successes. The partnership group members believed this approach lent credibility to their efforts and encouraged people to buy in to the initiative. Responding to local concerns has become an ongoing process, and the community coalition continues to be an important way for the community to meet its needs.

As a result of the initiative, the police officer assigned to this area began spending as much of his time as possible in the community. This helped make residents feel safer and contributed to a more positive image for the police. A neighbourhood foot patrol was established—staffed by resident volunteers—that also helped to make residents feel safer. Another key activity was hosting community events that brought service providers and community members together, for example, summer family barbecues and springtime campaigns to spruce up the neighbourhood. All these activities are designed to make the neighbourhood a better place to live. The focus has been on decreasing residents' fear of crime and increasing pride in the neighbourhood. The key has been giving residents a voice and working with them so that they feel that they have some say over what happens in their community.

The service providers have worked hard to make accessing support and needed services easier. They have benefited from the coalition as well since they have learned how to cooperate and work together to meet mutual needs. A child protection worker stated quite forcefully that he had never been more effective in his work nor felt more valued than when he worked as part of the coalition (Caputo et al. 2001). It provided him with the opportunity to contribute to the community in ways that had not happened before when he was perceived very negatively by community residents as someone who was there to take away their children. He said that he is now able to meet and talk to community residents and work with other service providers to help families.

The coalition is anchored around a core group of agencies and individuals including school, police, social services, and a community coordinator; 24 agencies and individuals are involved to varying degrees. It also includes representatives from different ethnic groups in the community. However, to reach this point was very challenging. First, the core group had to figure out how to get other groups and agencies to work together. No formal process existed for doing this. They had to develop such criteria for participation as being committed to the neighbourhood, having front-line involvement in the community, being in a strategic position to address a problem or issue within the community, and being motivated to be part of the coalition. The coalition sought to include individuals who were prepared to take action, not just plan for it.

While the coalition began with a group of dedicated community agency workers, staff turnover in the participating agencies has been high. This led to other challenges, including how to continue to engage new workers, who are invited to join and to learn about the coalition and its goals. This does not always work as agencies have not always been willing to give their staff the time needed to attend meetings. In some cases, new staff members are not interested in working with the coalition, preferring instead to work on their own. However, the coalition offers participants the opportunity to realize the positive benefits of cooperation. This encourages workers to get involved and stay involved. Some workers have taken personal time to be involved because they see the benefits of working together even if their agencies do not.

One of the biggest challenges for the coalition members has been sharing confidential information with each other. There are legal barriers to information sharing, including protecting the privacy of individuals. At the same time, it has quickly become clear to those working in the community that information sharing is very beneficial. It allows problems to be identified earlier and new issues to be addressed as they emerge. Information sharing also makes it easier to work collaboratively in comparison to the more SILOED approaches many members had used in the past in which each agency worked independently of the others.

Trust has allowed these service providers to begin to work together more effectively and to share what information they can. The process of building trust between and among service providers and with residents has been fundamental to the work of the coalition. Trust is something built over time and is based on respecting confidentiality and on partners following through on promises. Trust allows the service providers in the coalition to find ways to work together within the legal and ethical contexts of their professions and while respecting the confidentiality of their clients.

Neoliberal State Power and the Move toward the Community

If the move toward the community was easy for the state, simply inserting the word community into programs and having them run by agencies or groups that work or live in a community might be enough. However, as we have seen, the move toward community and responsibilization is not easy. Providing funding for programs and services in communities and having this funding be effective is very challenging, especially if the perception in the community is that the state is setting the agenda at a distance. As we have seen, when an initiative is completely external to a community, as in Case Study 4.3, there is often considerable activity but little sustainability. However, when local groups organize and seek funding, as was the case in Marionville in Case Study 4.1, and when there is a good fit between funding and locally defined needs, then state programs can play a critical role in community-based initiatives. But even in these cases the appeal of funding can be limited. As the Saint John example showed (Case Study 4.2), community-based groups can be concerned that state funding means that there are strings attached and that the state will attempt to steer the process.

In addition to the challenges that exist when the state attempts to set the agenda for communities through funding, the power dynamics that are at play in communities make it difficult for the state to impose partnership requirements. The funding process can also result in programs failing because groups or agencies are unwilling to work in partnership and share power (see Case Study 4.4). Further, partnerships not only require a willingness to share decision-making and other forms of power, they also require groups to find ways of working together. Working together requires overcoming a range of barriers such as information sharing and staff turnover that can result in efforts collapsing, even when there is good will and commitment (see Case Study 4.5). Finally, changes in state funding levels for social programs have meant that there is a shrinking pot of money for which groups and organizations must compete.

Chapter 5

THE CONSEQUENCES OF NEOLIBERAL FUNDING REGIMES

Introduction

In the move toward the community, the neoliberal state has attempted to use its power over funding to control the local agenda. The decision by a community group or organization to take state funding is an important one since it suggests that they are willing to serve as state agents and allow the state to steer. However, as the Saint John Resiliency Centre example shows (see Case Study 4.2), many in the community are concerned that using state funds means that decisions regarding what will be done will reflect the political agenda of the funders rather than their own.

This chapter explores the role of state funding in greater detail, with a specific focus on how the shift from core funding to short-term project funding has affected the delivery of programs and services in communities. Many community-based groups and organizations are becoming **PROJECT JUNKIES** because they are forced to pursue a seemingly endless series of short-term projects in order to keep their doors open, retain their staff, and serve their clients. They have to continuously reinvent themselves and their programs in order to fit funding requirements set by the state.

Funding strategies for community-based activities under neoliberal governments in Canada have gone through several iterations. Two key features are particularly important. First is the shift to short-term project funding. Second is the introduction of additional requirements related to evaluation, which has turned efficiency and accountability into ends in themselves. In addition to these features, we consider broader issues related to funding, specifically how funding shapes the issue of the ownership of problems. This includes both competition within communities among groups and the reluctance of various groups and organizations to accept ownership for complex problems.

From Core Funding to Short-Term Project Funding

Under successive neoliberal governments in Canada, funding for community-based activities has shifted from core funding to project funding aimed at specific issues, populations, and purposes. This shift has been described as "a complex set of changes ... that are coming together under a new funding regime" (Canadian Council on Social Development 2003, 39). Core funding had provided a stable, long-term source of funds for those providing programs and services in the community, typically under contract to the state. This allowed them to plan and provide programs and services on an ongoing basis. Under project funding, the state no longer assumes the responsibility for providing a range of programs and services. Instead, it seeks to meet its responsibilities in various service areas by funding a series of time-limited projects. Rather than providing stable and sustainable funding to meet its obligations, including those related to the social safety net, the neoliberal state has replaced this universal approach by short-term targeted funding in areas that match its policy priorities.

This neoliberal project funding regime has had a significant impact on many groups and organizations working in communities and influenced the way they operate. This is especially true for small single-issue community organizations who have been unable to compete for the available project funding. Many lack the ability to write successful project proposals, while others do not meet various state funding criteria. In one initiative, The Streetlifestyle Study, 27 agencies came together to discuss the issue of high-risk youth in the community and what might be done to ensure their safety and well-being. At a subsequent meeting four months later, there were seven fewer people at the community table since their smaller not-for-profit organizations had closed their doors, unable to secure the funding needed to keep operating (Caputo et al. 1997).

Larger organizations with the internal resources to pursue project funding are generally more successful than smaller ones in securing state funds. Many have been able to establish control over an issue or program area (e.g., seniors, youth, or homelessness) often to the exclusion of their competitors in the community. As a result, the successful organizations are able to grow ever larger while others shrink or fade away entirely. However, being successful is not without its consequences since the larger organizations face increasing pressure to secure a steady stream of state funding. They may find it necessary to expand into new areas, as funding for one issue dries up and other funding priorities are established. Over time, this can result in one large agency providing a range of programs and services to the exclusion of smaller groups and organizations. The dependency of these large organizations on state funding can make them a virtual extension of the state.

Project funding can also commercialize agencies, forcing them to act like profit-making organizations even though they are not-for-profit entities. This occurs because project funding has specific criteria, accountability structures, and goals that change the nature of the activities provided as well as the way they are delivered. Project funding can also lead to a potential loss of autonomy since it becomes increasingly difficult for client organizations to criticize the government as this would be akin to biting the hand that feeds you (Richmond and Shields 2004). As a result, criticism and debate are muted, and many local concerns fall off the funding table.

Further, innovation and programs tailored to meet local needs are discouraged because state-approved model programs and best practices are promoted by funding agencies. This is the case even when these models or best practices are imported from other communities or even other countries where conditions can differ markedly from those faced by local communities. In a risk averse environment where accountability is at a premium, best practices represent a safer bet for the state than something created locally over which the state has little or no control.

The federal state also uses project funding to influence the local agenda in areas of provincial/territorial jurisdiction. These programs are aimed at increasing local responsibility in key areas where the state is transferring funds to the provinces. If they are successful, they allow the federal state to influence responsibilization into areas outside their jurisdiction. While the federal state is limited by jurisdictional restraints from acting directly in areas such as education and health, they can sponsor pilot projects, which are used (ostensibly) to test new ideas and spur innovation. In funding a pilot project, the state hopes that the value of the project will eventually be recognized so that someone—the host agency itself, another voluntary sector organization, the business community, a philanthropic society, or another level of government—will step in and take responsibility for providing ongoing funding. The ideal is that useful programs will be recognized and steps will be taken to make them sustainable. The benefit to the central state is reduced cost obtained by transferring responsibility to a cheaper alternative.

How do community-based groups get state funding? First, they have to become aware of a request for proposals. Then, they have to prepare and submit a proposal for review. The review process is often protracted, taking many months to unfold. In some cases, agencies may be required to revise and resubmit their proposals. Importantly, there are no guarantees that projects will be funded so that agencies may invest large amounts of time, energy, and resources into preparing proposals and end up with nothing to show for their efforts. Chances for success can be shaped by whether an agency has the resources, knowledge, skills, and expertise required to develop a competitive proposal. These resources vary considerably across organizations, and this has contributed to a shifting landscape favouring those groups and agencies that have a greater capacity to prepare competitive proposals, including such things as a professional and well-educated staff familiar with the proposal writing process. Grant writing workshops have flourished as agencies work toward developing the required skill sets to successfully apply for funding.

In preparing funding applications, community-based groups and organizations quickly find that they are highly restricted in how they can use the funds. In most cases, the federal government will not allow project funds to cover administrative costs. This typically includes both the costs of preparing an application and overhead costs such as office space, telephone, computer systems, and secretarial support. The terms of program funding usually restrict the use of funds to paying for the actual delivery of programs or services. There are no funds to pay someone to coordinate the program or to deal with the various community partners that are required to be involved.

Ironically, while the state wants these programs and services to be sustainable, the restrictions placed on how project funds can be used severely limits the possibility of this outcome. Our research into sustainability indicates, for example, that coordination is a critical factor. If a program is to survive beyond the short-term state funding period, having a coordinator is one of the most important elements for promoting sustainability. Project funding criteria results in a dynamic in which projects are funded, complete their terms, and then cease to exist because there are no resources to ensure that they can continue. Agencies must apply for new project funding in the hope that their programs, services, or target populations are still funding priorities for the state and that they can be funded a second time for a project, since project funding is typically provided to help new initiatives; that is, pilot projects are normally funded only once.

In this type of funding environment, community groups and agencies find themselves struggling to secure their next funded project, moving from one pot of soft money to another. At the end of each project, no matter how successful, agencies agonize about what to do with project staff (who are usually hired on term contracts linked to the duration of the project funding). Staff are often lost along with the skills they acquired to run the project, the on-the-ground knowledge they have gained, and the connections to people both in other agencies and within the community. The agency is left to seek new funding and begin again from scratch. In being forced to do this over and over, the agency becomes a project junkie.

Case Study 5.1: A Case Study of Project Funding: Crime Prevention through Social Development

The shift to project funding has had a variety of consequences, as illustrated in a case study of crime prevention funding. The case study is based on data gathered from interviews with 172 front-line workers from community-based groups and organizations that had received or applied for federal crime prevention funding through the National Strategy on Community Safety and Crime Prevention (the Strategy). The Strategy emerged as neoliberalism was expanding in Canada.

> [S]ince 1992–93, program spending at both the federal and provincial levels has fallen. Before the onset of the recession, total federal program spending including transfers to individuals and governments was 15.8 per cent of GDP. In 1992–93, it reached 17.5 per cent. It has subsequently fallen to 12.2 per cent in the 1999–2000 fiscal year and is projected to fall further. The federal government claims that program spending is now at a 50-year low. Between 1989–90 and 1999–2000, transfers to individuals have fallen from 4.6 per cent to 4.1 per cent of GDP; transfers to other governments—monies that fund social assistance, health care, post-secondary education and community services—have fallen from 3.6 per cent to 2.2 per cent of GDP. (Canadian Factbook on Poverty 2000).

As the government was reducing spending on social services and programs, it expanded its spending on crime prevention. This made the Strategy an important source of funding for many groups and organizations working in communities. Agencies seeking to maintain or expand programs in the face of cuts began to look for alternative sources of funding, and many discovered that the Strategy was providing funds in areas with broadly defined parameters.

The Strategy has by most accounts been a highly successful enterprise. Thousands of community-based crime prevention projects have been funded since its inception in 1994. The scope and variety of these activities provide important insights into how communities and community-based groups and organizations responded to a difficult funding environment.

There are three general approaches to crime prevention: situational crime prevention, crime prevention through environmental design, and crime prevention through social development (CPSD). The first encourages such strategies as better surveillance, putting bars on windows of homes or businesses, and installing larger and more effective locks. The second calls for alterations to the physical environment through the deployment of better lighting and the removal of bushes or other landscape features that restrict visibility. In contrast, CPSD addresses the underlying social and economic root causes of crime and victimization. Many CPSD activities are directed toward youth and seek to prevent or reduce the risk of youth becoming involved in or of continuing their involvement in crime by seeking to address the challenges they face in their lives. Most of the 172 groups and agencies interviewed were involved in CPSD projects. This gave them latitude to define their particular issue as one that reflected the Strategy's mandate. Only a small number reported being involved in projects related to situational crime prevention or crime prevention through environmental design.

Given its broad definition, a CPSD approach can embrace a wide range of activities as long as they address factors identified as risks for involvement in criminal activity. They included educational programs, social housing programs, shelters for abused women, shelters for homeless youth, parenting classes, programs for the identification of and early intervention with high-risk children and youth, and programs aimed at meeting a number of other social needs such as recreation and employment. Other crime prevention activities were bike rodeos, beach clean-ups, and providing placements for serving community service hours. The link between such programs and criminal activity was disparate. As one respondent said, "there are lots of programs but not all are [directly] geared to crime prevention. They *could* lead to prevention" (Canadian Factbook on Poverty 2000). Agencies adopting a CPSD approach reported that they became involved in crime prevention activities primarily because the activities they proposed fit both their vision or their mandate as well as the funding criteria of the Strategy. They had been providing support to clients as part of the social safety net prior to their involvement in crime prevention. As the social safety net was being dismantled and what were once entitlement programs were being cut, agencies had to seek alternative means of support, and crime prevention offered an opportunity for them to do this.

Consider the example of one community that had a long history of social development activities that were coordinated through a city-wide central council. As budgets for social programming were cut, the council responded by trying to enhance community development and to maintain its existing social support system by altering how activities were funded. Since fixed funds were no longer available to support a long-running breakfast program, it applied for funding for a project that tapped into the government's concern with youth at risk by linking poor nutrition to poor school performance, and poor school performance to later criminality. This allowed those running school breakfast programs to apply for funding as a crime prevention activity.

Receiving Strategy funding for CPSD projects, however, was not without consequences. Some programs had to be changed to fit funding criteria. Further, while Strategy funding made projects possible, it also resulted in a lack of stability since these were typically soft funds with time-limited periods and available only on a project-by-project basis. Once project funding ended, activities did not, generally, persist. Thus, while the government had built up an array of participating agencies, these ties were fleeting, making the impact of the funding short-lived.

The case study of Strategy Projects pinpointed concerns about who was and was not able to secure funding. While community crime prevention ostensibly meant that community members should have a key role in defining what should be done and how to implement their own solutions, funding practices favoured existing agencies who had knowledge, experience, and capacity over local community groups. In addition, the funding process itself required considerable expertise, skill, and investment of time and energy to prepare proposals. This was a concern for all the agencies, but it was a particular concern for Aboriginal communities where the existing infrastructure was often more limited. While the need in their communities was relatively easy for them to document, a lack of expertise in writing grant proposals meant that Aboriginal communities often failed to secure funds.

Groups working within communities had other concerns as well. For example, some were concerned that local and national priorities did not coincide; as one person said, "[while] it's nice to do things at a national level, the community needs can be different. I may talk about things [that are needed] in this community that would not be discussed in Montreal" (personal communication). Although there was considerable activity around crime prevention at the time of the study, its quality was another matter. Many people had never done crime prevention work before so their work was of questionable effectiveness. Indeed, while many programs were being run across the country, there were few details and even fewer rigorous assessments of the impact they had on crime, on the community, or even on individual participants. The result was that while the government has been successful in promoting the notion of CPSD, the experience that communities have had with crime prevention has been far more complex. Money was spent, projects came and went, but it was not clear what impact, if any, this has had over the longer term. There are impacts on agencies—they may find they have to spend considerable resources to get funding, putting in multiple project proposals to a variety of different government departments, and they may have to shift or bend their mandates to qualify for funding. There are impacts on communities—some have had a modicum of success in sustaining their community-based activity once project funding ends. But, overall, as we have seen, the state has created a generation of organizations that are project junkies.

Evaluation

As we noted above, in early iterations the neoliberal funding regime did not include the specific requirement for agencies to assess the impact or effectiveness of programs. As a result, there was considerable activity but very little evidence of effects. As the neoliberal regime has developed and matured, accountability measures have been built into the program funding process. This includes requiring agencies seeking funding to provide measures of effectiveness and to have their programs evaluated. Accountability through detailed evaluations has become an important way for the state to exercise increasing control over those receiving funding.

Evaluation has had complex consequences. Evaluators are supposed to assess the impact of a program or project. This has created a number of dilemmas for the groups and agencies running the projects as well as for the state itself. First, it has proven difficult for agencies to find and retain both dedicated staff and external evaluators. While there has been an increase in the number of evaluators and the establishment of organizations seeking to accredit evaluators, agencies have limited expertise in selecting them. Further, additional and sometimes significant funds are required to pay for the mandated evaluations. The state has passed some of these costs onto agencies and has also sought to reduce rising costs by reducing the number of projects funded. Finally, evaluations provide information on the effectiveness of projects. In some cases, the evaluation may find that that a program has not met its intended goals. While this may be perceived as a failure of the program, it may actually reflect that the desired impact cannot be achieved under short-term project funding. In other cases, a key finding of project evaluation is the unmet needs of clients. While the state can try to pass responsibility for these shortcomings onto the agencies providing the service, many evaluations point out that the deficiencies lie not with the program but with the overall system.

Given that evaluation poses many challenges, it is important to ask why the state has placed the additional requirement to evaluate within project funding? Evaluating the impact of a project makes good fiscal sense for neoliberal governments. In shifting responsibility for addressing needs and problems to the community, the state can use mechanisms such as evaluation to base decisions on how to proceed. In 2000, it was alleged that government funds were not being properly accounted for in projects funded by Human Resources Development Canada (HRDC) (Phillips and Levasseur 2004). While this was certainly a catalyst for the government insisting on evaluation, there had already been a significant push for more accountability for projects. However, the HRDC controversy has probably shaped the emphasis on oversight being primarily fiscal in nature. One aspect of this is impact measurement—assessing the impact of the project.

To be eligible for funding, groups and agencies have to include an evaluation plan as part of their proposal. As a result, there are fewer funds for projects and increased pressure on groups and agencies to establish their success. The success aspect is important: when a current project ends, funding has to be found from a new source to keep the agency going; failure to prove success may be used to deny the funding. In addition, the new evaluation requirements may work to limit the types of projects that will be funded since positive evaluations favour projects with short-term measurable results. Further, to the extent that evaluation requires collecting data on and from an agency, issues of client confidentiality and ethics pose challenges. It is also not clear that the state has the resources to audit these evaluations in any meaningful way.

In an experience typical of evaluation challenges, one of the authors worked on a project evaluating the impact of training high school students in alternate dispute resolution. The project was state funded and had an evaluation component.

As funding was time-limited and resources were scarce, the decision was made to evaluate changes in attitudes before and after training by students who used violence to resolve disputes. The evaluation—indeed the project itself—was deemed extremely successful. The short-term measures of success included a significant decline in pro-violence attitudes, increased awareness of alternate strategies to resolve conflicts, and a commitment by youth to walk away from potential fights. To further support the claim that the project had an impact on its subject community, data were also collected on the number of fights in the school and the number of suspensions and expulsions. These showed that the school atmosphere was much improved, but they could not be directly attributed to the training as there were a number of initiatives going on at the same time, and they were for the entire school, not just for the youth who had received the training. When the agency sought additional funding, they were told that while the funder saw short-term change, it was not convinced of the program's effectiveness because of the lack of long-term outcomes. Funding was denied, and the program ended.

Revisiting the Concept of Community

We began this book by pointing out that the concept of community has received increasing attention in both public and political discourse. We asked a series of questions about how the concept is defined and who or what is the community. We then noted that the community has become an important site for neoliberal policy and practice as the state has attempted to download responsibility for social programs through its move toward the community. In order to better understand what has been happening on the ground, we reviewed the challenges faced by the state in identifying with whom to work in communities and how different definitions of community can emerge in state-funded projects.

The question of who the community is remains problematic. As we have seen, the face of the community has, in many case, become agencies and non-government organizations. This is linked, in part, to the state's previous history of engaging agencies to deliver social programs and, in part, to identifying the community as a geographic area where the state has engaged community actors to deliver programs and services. Under this definition of community, people who work in a particular area are identified as members of that community and are, in consequence, able to speak on its behalf. There is, however, little critical consideration of the fact that these professionals may work for organizations that have their own agendas, goals, and values. Such issues are important because much of the work done at the local level claims that it is, in fact, community-based even when no community residents are involved. So, groups and agencies speak for the community. However, a community does not speak with one voice. As Kumar (2005) notes, different advocates can have quite differing ideas about who and what the community is and what it needs. Agencies may indeed be part of a community and well able to speak on its behalf. However, this still begs the question of who is the community and where community residents fit in this equation.

Two issues emerge from this discussion. First, the recognition of agencies as the face of the community has meant that community residents are displaced. This has been described as the hollowing out of the community. The second relates to the question of the power of agencies and organizations and their ability to claim ownership of particular issues (e.g., homelessness, violence) within a community. We discuss this in terms of who owns the problem.

The Hollowing Out of the Community

Hollowing out occurs when responsibility for managing local concerns has increasingly been downloaded to the community, community-based agencies, rather than residents or those with a value and/or moral connection to the community, have become the face of the community for many state programs and services. As a result, the state, rather than the people, determines what the community needs. Is this what has happened to community under neoliberalism in Canada?

Many features that Orsini identifies as a hollowing out of the community are present. For example, agencies seeking state funding have to "tailor their agendas to the needs and priorities of the state" and failing to do so may have a profound impact on their ability to continue to operate. Groups who receive funding are required to "navigate a complicated maze of government policies and practices to qualify for support" (Orsini 2006, 24–25). Further, the cost in time and resources of applying for funding can mean that smaller organizations may not have the capacity to make applications or to meet the requirements to administer the funding in a way that conforms to state expectations. This effectively limits who applies for funding and who gets considered as a representative of the community.

There is intense competition among groups to be accepted by the state as governmental. Orsini (2006, 33) argues that some agencies, including those that engage in advocacy work (such as women's centres), receive less funding than those that provide health and social services—priority issues in state policy. This situation creates dilemmas for front-line agencies. Those who do not receive funding are less able to assist marginal groups, and those that do receive funding are faced, even when they are supportive of programs that assist marginal groups, with having to match their programs to state priorities.

However, the hollowing out of community is not easily achieved nor is it necessarily complete. There are two key challenges: one relates to the willingness of communities to accept state funding and the other to the ability of the state to sustain activity. As the case examples in Chapters 3 and 4 indicate, not all groups and organizations are willing to accept state funding. Indeed, in Saint

John (Case Study 4.2), the youth and their families seeking or needing support worked with local agencies, all under the pressure of funding cuts, to produce a powerful partnership that allowed them to define and respond to local needs. This was not a hollowed-out community; rather, it was a community where those defined as in need of services formed a key part of a community-based response. Indeed, the study of sustained activity shows that the most long-lived and effective programs are those that deal with problems that are meaningful to those living and working in the community and in which there are partnerships between residents or those receiving services and the agencies providing the programs. The state provides funding and attempts to mandate priorities, but success and sustainability require local ownership and local meaning.

Who Owns the Problem?

As noted in Chapter 4, a key challenge of working at the community level revolves around the exercise of power. Power struggles among agencies have an impact on how issues are defined and addressed. In the process, some groups are placed in the centre of the action while others are marginalized. The case studies in that chapter provided some interesting examples of how competition between organizations over turf can marginalize and centralize groups with respect to their recognition as the face of the community.

One such example, which we discuss below, arose over the question of who owns the problem of violence. As you will see, this is not a simple question, but one that raises many important issues. For example, is violence a women's issue? A men's issue? A community issue? Does it belong to a specific cultural, ethnic, or religious group? Is it a legal issue restricted to the police and the courts? The question of ownership can be asked about almost every community issue. For instance, if the issue is violence in the community, the problem can be identified in numerous ways. If youth crime and victimization are identified as the problem, does this mean that the bulk of the community's resources should go to addressing this as opposed to other concerns such as violence against women? At the same time, once a problem has been identified, there may be a number of groups competing over who has a right to provide services. Ownership of the problem is important because it means that a group or organization has the right to define what the problem is, what solutions and actions need to be taken, and where the funding or other support should go. When a problem has been identified within a community, different groups and organizations will, potentially, have different interpretations of what the nature of the problem is and what solutions are required. When a group or organization is identified as having ownership of a problem, this often means it is able to attract funding and have an impact on the local agenda.

Who owns the problem can also lead to inaction—to nothing being done. In some cases, the various groups or agencies most closely identified with a service area may back away from taking responsibility for a difficult or complex issue because it will be very expensive for them to act. In this context, deciding who owns the problem really means who is legally responsible for paying for the services and supports that are needed. When the problem is complex and multi-faceted, service providers can avoid taking ownership by defining the problem narrowly or identifying it as the responsibility of others. The consequences of agencies refusing to own a problem can be serious for individual clients and the community as a whole since important concerns can go unaddressed.

Case Study 5.2: Contesting Ownership

In 1994 a large Canadian city embarked on a community-wide initiative on youth violence. It began with a town hall meeting that the authors attended. It brought together over 600 people. More wanted to come, but there was no space to accommodate them in the meeting room. Those in attendance decided to conduct a needs assessment and then develop a plan to respond to the issue. Task groups were formed. However, early in the initiative, a key conflict emerged. A local women's group was concerned that too much attention was being paid to youth violence and that the profile of violence against women in the community might be diminished as a result. They argued that programming and funding would shift to youth violence, leaving those addressing violence against women with fewer resources. They asserted that they owned the problem of violence against women and that the community-wide initiative would undermine their ability to garner attention and support for initiatives addressing this problem.

The organizing group persisted in pursing the issue of youth violence. They too asserted some ownership of the problem of violence and rejected the claim that, in seeking support for their issue, other agencies would be harmed. There was considerable friction, and the dispute became quite public and personal. In addition to raising concerns in the meetings, the group dealing with violence against women began to lobby actively against the community-wide initiative and to attack the leaders of the initiative personally in their discussions with groups and organizations, including both local and national funders. The community-wide initiative eventually dissipated as people wanted to avoid conflict, but a core group continued to work on the issue of youth violence. This group was extremely successful in gaining access to state funding aimed at youth violence and in developing much-needed programs.

This turf war illustrates a key challenge that community-based groups and organizations face—there are only limited resources available and government funding programs that are project focused often put groups and organizations in competition. These competitions have long-term consequences. Successful groups may grow and be able to dominate others. They become recognized as the "go to" agencies, which may increase their chances of funding success in the future. This can lead to the demise of competing groups and agencies since there is less funding available for them.

The fall-out from this conflict was interesting. One agency emerged as the key player working with youth and youth violence. It was able to parlay this status into a massive expansion of its agency to work closely with federal, provincial, and municipal governments to deliver key government programs. It became the largest service provider for youth in the city. The women's group continued to work on the issue of family violence but was not able to grow its profile within the community. It continued to advocate on behalf of women and on family violence issues, but it remained small and had access to much fewer resources than what was provided to the youth-serving agency.

Owning the problem is complex. State intervention in the process can have a profound impact on what happens in communities. This occurs through a process in which particular groups and agencies are identified and selected as the voice of a community on a particular issue. When the state is sensitive to who owns an issue, it will direct funding to them. As a result, others providing programs and services in the same area may be left with a smaller pool of resources and funding for their work. However, as we have just seen, sometimes such efforts can lead to intense conflict. The question of who owns the problem is all about power and struggles over turf, and reflects the fact that the state is only one among many players that exercise power in communities.

Case Study 5.3: Refusing Ownership

In contrast to struggles over who owns the problem, there are situations in which no one wants to own a problem. Whether this is due to indifference or because the issue is too complex, time-consuming, or costly, the failure to engage with a problem also has profound and possibly devastating impacts on communities.

For example, between 1980 and 2002 as many as 60 women disappeared from Vancouver's Downtown Eastside neighbourhood (Cameron 2007). These disappearances did not go unnoticed. The women's families, groups working in the neighbourhood, and others reported them missing and requested action. While reports were taken, little was done. Even as groups began to suspect that there was a serial killer working in the area, no one acted. Who owned the problem? Was this a personal problem—owned by individual families as they searched frantically for missing sisters, daughters, neices, and mothers? Was this a problem owned by groups and agencies serving the community? These groups and agencies had no resources to search for the women. They could and did warn others of the risk, but the exact nature of the risk was unknown. Was it a police problem? The police took no ownership. They had no bodies and viewed the women, many of whom worked in the sex trade, as a transient unconnected population who moved on without warning. No one owned the problem. Eventually, Robert William

Pickton, a pig farmer who lived just outside the city, was arrested, tried, and convicted for six murders, with other charges still pending. There is currently an inquiry underway into why it took so long for anyone to act. It has received requests from multiple groups and agencies for legal standing, including the Department of Justice, the RCMP, the Vancouver Police, the City of Vancouver, the Crown Counsel's Office, Amnesty International, and the BC Civil Liberties Association. In addition, the Assembly of First Nations and the Union of BC Chiefs are asking for standing as well as the Women's Equality and Security Coalition, which includes 11 community groups (Canadian Press, 8 December 2010). Suddenly, everyone has a stake and some ownership of the problem. As the inquiry gets underway, all these groups are seeking to shape how the problem will be defined and perhaps who or what was to blame for the failure to act.

The question of who owns the problem is basically a funding issue. It is about what the state is willing to fund, who is able to define the dimensions of a problem and the strategies for responding to it, and who is willing and able to address it. Under current neoliberal practices, concerns have been raised about the ability of groups in Aboriginal communities and women's groups to have their problems recognized and funded. The Pickton case is a vivid example of this situation.

Discussion

The shift to a project-funding approach under successive neoliberal govern-ments and the addition of increased oversight through evaluation (among other mechanisms) has had a profound impact at the community level. Short-term funding has led many agencies to become project junkies always moving on to new issues and programs just to stay afloat. In the process, there is little, if any, scope for innovation or advocacy.

Evaluation has impacted on what agencies do and how they do it. It has increased accountability and transparency with respect to how funds are used, what occurs in programs, and what the outcomes will be. However, evaluation requirements have also seriously affected how not-for-profit and voluntary sector organizations provide services, the activities they undertake, and the clients they serve. They have been required to expand their documentation and increase their use and reporting of statistics measuring success. Further, outcomes have become increasingly focused on specific measurable results that have to be achieved within the funding mandate—a time frame that usually lasts between one and three years. This can be challenging for groups and organizations that provide services that are intended to have long-term consequences such as those working to treat violent offenders or providing support for those struggling with addictions. The need for immediate and measurable results has made it difficult for groups to get support for programs that focus on long-term outcomes.

The hollowing out of communities has resulted in agencies and organizations based in communities being increasingly defined as the community and residents are either ignored or assigned a secondary role. These agencies have their own *raisons d'être* that are not aligned with the interests or needs of community residents nor often with other service providers. The need to secure state funding is so crucial to these agencies that they often bend to the will of the state in setting community needs and priorities (Orsini 2006, 24). This complicates their relationship with the communities they are supposed to be serving.

Thus, when community-based organizations are accepted by the government as the community, they must, if they seek government funding, respond to government directives to support their agencies' existence. This makes funding a key aspect in shaping what happens on the ground. For example, through its funding programs, the government determines priority groups and concerns. The funding priority process creates dilemmas for front-line agencies whose programs assist marginal groups. They must either refuse funding and then not have the resources they need for their programs or pursue funding that addresses the needs of the priority groups identified by the state rather than the groups they themselves identify.

Owning the problem is a challenge that emerges as a further expression of the state's control over funding. Groups and agencies strive to own problems as a means of getting funding. This can lead to intense conflict within communities and the marginalization of those groups and organizations who lose these battles. The ones that survive often go on to become large, dominant agencies with considerable power. Several contemporary critics have raised concerns over the potentially negative consequences that may occur as a result of competing or conflicting power groups operating at the community level (Cohen 1985; Garland 2001; Graddy and Morgan 2006; O'Malley 1992; Pavlich 1996; Rose 1996), such as the development of local-level oligarchies that deploy undemocratic, unrepresentative networks of special interests (Geddes 2006). In some cases, these oligarchies can marginalize various groups in a community, especially those in the at-risk categories (Pavlich 1996; Crawford 1999). The diverse power nodes that exist at the local level have meant that the move toward the community is not easy or automatic.

We must therefore be cautious in trying to understand what has happened as a result of the move toward the community by the state. There are many social problems that are complex and challenging or that no one wants to address. In these cases, the issues or problems may go unaddressed because neither the state nor community residents are willing or able to act. In such cases, the move toward the community has not resolved the situation but may actually have made it worse.

The actions of the neoliberal state—despite its intentions—are neither universally positive nor universally negative. As we have seen in the examples and case studies above, there is often give and take with community-level actors.

However, the move toward the community has resulted in profound changes for how community agencies do business, for the problems they address, and for the clients they serve. Community groups and agencies alike have to negotiate with the neoliberal state in this changing context.

Chapter 6

REFLECTIONS

This book considers why there has been a downloading of responsibility to the community under neoliberalism and indicates some of the consequences of this shift for those living and working in communities across the country. We began by discussing the appeal of the concept of community both for the state and for the public and why it has proven so popular as a policy instrument. The impact of successive neoliberal regimes on the provision of social programs and services was also examined, along with the particular tactics and strategies employed by the state to control the local agenda. Throughout our discussion, we kept a focus on the dynamics involved in attempting to set the local agenda. In this final chapter we reflect on these discussions and consider the implications they have for our understanding of what is happening today and what the future may hold.

Community studies have had a long history, and the appeal of a concept that suggests familiar and friendly relationships among people who know each other and share important values and beliefs has been a persistent theme. This romantic view of community evokes a feeling of nostalgia for a fondly remembered past even though that past may or may not ever have existed. It also makes people feel comfortable and hopeful that things can be better if only they could return to old-style communities. While this is the appeal of both community and a promise of a return to community for the general public, it is very different from the way the concept is being used by the state.

Why has the concept of community garnered so much attention over the past few decades? The answer, as we have seen, is neoliberal policy. Globally, neoliberal states have deregulated, divested, and reduced or eliminated service provision while local communities, groups, and individuals have felt the impact. In particular, the state has downloaded program delivery to local levels while attempting to maintain regulatory control for itself. There are fewer resources available to support a social safety net, and there is a push for local groups and organizations to find ways of sustaining state-sponsored initiatives. At the same time, the state is not providing funds to support core agency functions—paying for a building, equipment, supplies, and the administrative staff to coordinate and lead initiatives. Agencies working on the ground have been forced to form partnerships with each other in order to receive state funding and, in the process, have been asked to contribute their own resources—in-kind service, personnel, and even monetary resources. The state attempts to get more for less investment while maintaining control over what is happening locally. The state has tried to do this by leveraging its control over funding and funding requirements and through setting the agenda regarding the types of services and programs it will fund.

The concept of community has cachet for the state because it is a mechanism for downloading state responsibility for social supports while simultaneously sending a "good news" message that we are returning to a better way of doing things. One former prime minister referred to Canada as a "community of communities" (Clark 1979), evoking the idea that we are all embedded in a number of supportive communities. These communities, neoliberalism holds, are better able to provide the support and services people need than the state.

However, rather than the romanticized and nostalgic vision of a supportive community, what has emerged since the neoliberal shift is a hollowed-out community in which agencies and groups, rather than members of the community itself, are considered the face of the community. In part, this has been done by favouring agencies over residents in the funding process.

In this context, we looked at how neoliberal regimes have invoked the concept of community and how that is linked to an attempt to regulate how communities enact state-driven policy initiatives. Our analysis, however, did not stop there since it is our view that the state does not operate in a vacuum and that while it can promote various policy positions and funding programs, it does so within pre-existing structures and processes. For example, the remnants of the former welfare state continue to exist and have influence. Networks of well-established service providers hold considerable sway within communities. At the same time, many communities have a long history of actively identifying and meeting their own needs, and they are cautious when outsiders attempt to usurp this power. Throughout this book, our goal has been to take these competing interests into account and present a nuanced look at what has happened on the ground as the state has sought to engage communities as key players in responding to local needs and issues.

Who is the community? This is perhaps the most critical question that must be answered in exploring the move back to the community by the state. We began with the recognition that community is neither easily defined nor uniform across space and time. We then noted that once a community has been identified, its membership can encompass a wide variety of players, including people living in a particular location as well as those who share a commitment to a common set of values, beliefs, or interests. In the case of geographic communities, it can also include those working in communities such as community groups, representatives of the voluntary sector and not-for-profit organizations, and employees of state agencies providing programs and services.

In defining the community that will deliver programs there are two processes that must be negotiated. The first involves identifying the nature of the community (e.g., a geographic community or a cultural/ethnic community) and the second is identifying who are the members of that community. The state has chosen to adopt a geographic definition and to impose administrative boundaries. This sets some limits on who can claim membership. But there are few rules or restrictions related to membership and more importantly on who can speak or act on behalf of a community. Community members have included school principals and teachers; elders from ethnic communities; local business owners, representatives from social service agencies, local residents' associations, and municipal housing authorities; researchers; tenants of housing complexes; city officials and police officers; and members of church groups, senior citizens' groups, and other voluntary organizations.

Who becomes recognized as the face and voice of the community when there are so many potential actors? The examples from the case studies show that the definition of community that emerges in practice depends upon both the agenda—that is, the issue the state is seeking to address—and its willingness to recognize those seeking funding as appropriate agents to work on its behalf. The definition of community also depends on the actions of the state and the individuals, groups, agencies, and professionals within the boundaries of the defined community who identify with an issue. Struggles can develop within communities over funding and specifically over ownership of a particular problem or issue such as violence. While the state may impose clear criteria on its definition of community, who will respond to the state in any particular community can vary depending on which individuals, groups, or organizations are willing and able to do the work required.

Neoliberal states began their move toward the community by presenting it as a way of empowering those who would be sensitive to local conditions and needs. However, the state has done this while trying to retain its control over the social policy agenda. This includes making decisions about whether those applying for funding are suitable and by setting funding priorities for them. An important consideration for the state in this process, however, has been identifying groups or organizations that can actually do the work required, thus limiting its focus to whether or not the community groups or organizations seeking funding have the capacity to implement the policies and programs being promoted.

Thus, the state has chosen to work with selected community-based groups and organizations rather than grassroots community representatives. As a result, many state-funded community-based programs have not had any involvement of or input from community members. Groups and organizations are selected by the state for a number of reasons. One is willingness to implement state policy.

Another is the long history that has made the state familiar and comfortable with working with such organizations, many of which have come to be seen as being quasi-governmental. A third reason is that agencies have the capacity to develop proposals and the recognized knowledge and expertise to deliver programs. This approach makes sense when the goal of the state is to set the agenda and have a suitable group or agency act on its behalf. It makes less sense when the goal is to meet the needs and address the concerns of local residents. Agencies generally describe what they do as community-based, though this distinction may indeed be a hollow one since no one from the community is involved. Can agencies that depend on state funding be critical of state policies or advocate on behalf of the people they serve? Are these community-based agencies anything more than extensions of the state?

The discussion about who can and who cannot define themselves as members of the community is also important because it focuses our attention on who has the ability to identify issues or concerns and who decides what, if any, response will be made. If a program or service is community-based, members of that community should have some decision-making power. As we note throughout this book, during this period of neoliberalism the state has used a variety of strategies and tactics to retain the power to set the agenda—to steer—while passing the responsibility for meeting needs onto those working on the ground in communities. However, this has not been easy or straightforward. Some agencies, for example, apply for state funding as a strategy to meet their own agendas. This can pose challenges for the state, since the initiatives they fund often end when the project funding ends. This suggests that the state can steer the policy agenda only as long as they are willing to pay for it.

Some agencies apply for state funding as a strategic act. They address a local concern that the community has identified as important and apply for funds from state agencies whose mandates and focus match local concerns. These initiatives are more likely to be sustained because they are a concern to people who are willing to address them even when state funding ends. This suggests that in many cases the community will row—that is, follow the state agenda—only as long as state funding lasts or when the issue meets their own needs. As we saw in the case studies, some communities refuse to accept state funding because they recognize that it comes with strings attached.

The state has to find someone willing and able to do the work it wants done in the community. Community capacity is a key issue since many communities do not have the human, physical, and social capital needed to act. Under neoliberalism, the issue of community capacity has become a core concept to assess the ability of communities to take on the responsibility for meeting local needs as the state divests itself of the responsibility for providing various social supports. The notion of community capacity has proven difficult to define and measure. A lack of capacity means that a particular community does not have the ability to identify its needs nor to mobilize the necessary resources to meet them. Such a community cannot engage its members or secure the commitment of individuals and organizations. This is problematic for the neoliberal state, which has sought to develop capacity in order to have these communities enact its social policy. This is, in part, because communities that lack the capacity to act are also the communities that are typically facing serious and ongoing problems—high crime rates, ill health, addictions, poverty, violence. This represents a considerable challenge for the state since these communities and their problems often garner a great deal of media attention that reflects negatively on the government.

Neoliberalism has been quite dynamic, and the state has modified aspects of its programs and policies over time. In particular, it has introduced new criteria and management strategies to increase its oversight of projects. These measures include increased financial accountability and a requirement that state-funded projects be evaluated. This has placed increased strain on the already over-taxed local agencies seeking state funding.

Another strategy adopted by the state is to develop best practices which, it is assumed, can be transferred from community to community. This enhances the ability of the state to control the local agenda since it can select which programs it defines as a best practice. It can then require other communities to adopt this best practice if they are seeking state funding. The problem with this approach is that the state assumes that local conditions are not critical to program success and so continues to rely on a generic definition of community in which policy is enacted. In the process, the local has little meaning beyond the recognition that it is geographically located. The state ignores the important differences that exist in communities in its "one size fits all" approach. While this allows it greater control over the local agenda, it misses the key point that what it promotes may not be meaningful to communities nor meet local needs.

Within communities there has also been considerable activity under neoliberalism. Communities have come together to identify problems and seek ways to fill the funding void left by the cuts to the social safety net. In general, this has been led by community-based agencies who find their funding seriously eroded. They have come together to discuss the issues, one of which is the struggle over who owns a problem in a community. Ownership of a problem gives agencies considerable ability to set the local agenda. Such conflicts have resulted in winners and losers and, in particular, the growth of some agencies and the marginalization of others.

While the political theory and philosophy underlying neoliberalism has informed much of what various neoliberal states do, experience has shown that intentions do not always translate into practice. What happens on the ground as a result of state actions, including policy priorities, is an empirical question. Through our research, we have discovered that in Canada the state's neoliberal policy approach has had complex and often contradictory outcomes. One of the most challenging is that state-funded programs have not been sustainable once state funding ends. This suggests that the local level is not buying in to the state's agenda. We have also seen an ongoing need to refine policies in order to address the concerns that have emerged in practice, especially as this relates to assisting communities to build their capacity to deliver programs and services. For example, the state has recognized that community capacity is not evenly spread across communities; as a result, there is uneven program delivery as well as communities that are excluded or unable to participate.

State funding programs have been a key element in shaping what programs and projects are run in many communities. Among their numerous consequences is turning many agencies into project junkies. Having to rely on time-limited and project-specific funding has proven detrimental for those providing programs and services as well as those receiving these services. When funding ends, programs typically cease to exist because no one is able or willing to step in. As a result, while the state is trying to use pilot or demonstration projects to set its agenda, it has little to show for its efforts. At the same time, there is frustration within the communities as agencies search for other sources of funding in order to continue serving their clients.

The funding process has many flaws. Some agencies have been forced to dramatically alter their mandates in order to secure funding that will allow them to keep their doors open. Many are concerned about the time it takes to prepare proposals and the delays in hearing whether they have been successful. The requirements for evaluation have further complicated the funding process and made it more challenging for those preparing proposals. But agencies find themselves locked into the funding process of the state since they have few other options. As well as agencies, some communities are not able to apply for funding because they lack the necessary resources to do so. This has been the case with many Aboriginal, remote, and rural communities. The state has recognized this and struggled to find ways of assisting these communities, but there are simply too many communities in need of this type of assistance.

While the state is not controlling what happens at the local level, from the perspective of community-based groups and organizations its actions have had profound impact on how they work, what they work on, and what work gets done. But when the state attempts to set the agenda for communities, it faces challenges related to power dynamics that limit its success. The question of who owns a problem in a community can become the focus of considerable conflict as agencies see their issues and concerns marginalized or at risk of being marginalized by others seeking funding. This is particularly threatening to groups and agencies that define themselves as doing advocacy work. Such groups have been marginalized in many communities or they form their own networks to compete for funds.

From a community perspective, projects come and go while little seems to change. We discussed a number of reasons for this. It may be because the issue a project addresses is not of interest to the local community or because there are existing (competing) initiatives within the community that limit acceptance. Projects may also fail because there is insufficient capacity, including funds, to keep them going. What is truly frustrating at the community level occurs when a valued project ends with the funding agreement and there are no resources to carry on. This happens, in part, because agencies are forced to compete for short-term project funding and to continue on to the next funded project to keep their doors open. The state has not been oblivious to the loss of projects once funding ends, and it has sponsored research on what makes projects sustainable. Not surprisingly, the factors that contribute to sustainability include how meaningful the issues are to the community, the presence of strong local leadership, and the willingness to buy into the project. What is required is that communities have some input in determining what will happen locally—the state cannot dictate. In addition, sustainability requires some ongoing funding for administration, coordination, consultation, and communication functions. Project funding does not provide this type of support. In the absence of some local control and ongoing financial support, community level initiatives are unlikely to persist.

Some Final Thoughts

The community of neoliberal policy is neither the nostalgic community envisioned by Tönnies nor is it the regulated community of neoliberal ideology. The state has attempted to steer policy and practice through its use of funding regimes and regulatory mechanisms. In the process, the concept of community has been altered substantially—hollowed out and reduced to community agencies the state has identified as governmental. While this has allowed the state to set the policy agenda and to have others take responsibility for service delivery, its efforts have met with limited success. This is the case because the community has often been unable or unwilling to row.

So what is the situation today? On the one hand, neoliberal approaches to program delivery persist. However, they have become more nuanced and recognize, to varying degrees, the need to take local actors and conditions into account if policies are to be effective. On the other hand, the global economic crisis has seen many neoliberal states returning to deficit spending to avert a worldwide recession. Critics suggest that if neoliberalism had provided an effective mechanism for governing, the current financial crisis would not have happened. The return to Keynesian interventions may signal the reorientation of neoliberalism, which may have profound impacts in the future. The universalistic tendencies of the Keynesian welfare state had worked to level inequality and promote social inclusion, while neoliberal policy has contributed to an exacerbated polarization in society as the elite becomes increasingly rich while the bulk of the population has access to less and less. As a result of this growing polarization, social exclusion has become a serious issue internationally as conflicts rise and tensions among social groups increase. The consequences of social exclusion may well be on the agenda in the future in Canada and the United States as the gap between the rich and the poor and marginalized continues to grow.

Finally, local ownership, local control, and grassroots engagement remain important for most Canadians. In our research in communities in all regions of the country, it was clear that people are willing to come together to help each other and address common concerns, especially if this has to do with an issue that is meaningful to them, such as the safety of their children. This sense of civic responsibility has a firm legacy in many communities and continues to be important today. The willingness of people to address their own needs and concerns, however, is vastly different from many of the case studies that were concerned with the downloading of responsibility by the state for programs and services that form part of the social safety net. These programs and services had not been provided by the state as a result of its benevolence or good will. Instead, they reflect a long history of social struggles that saw basic rights enshrined in society as part of what it means to be a citizen. Laws protecting labour and the environment have been hard won as have social entitlements such as worker's compensation, old age pensions, publicly funded health care, and education. The attempt by the neoliberal state to try to shed its responsibility for the social safety net has met with varying degrees of success. In some cases, communities have acquiesced. In others, they have been opportunistic and used state funds in creative ways to meet their own interests. In still other cases, communities have resisted the downloading of responsibilities and challenged the state. The complexity of what has gone on must be taken into account if we are to develop a better understanding of what is happening on the ground in Canadian communities.

Glossary

ANOMIE: Refers to the state or condition of individuals or social groups in which people and groups feel aimless or lacking in purpose as a result of the lack of values and beliefs.

AUDIT TECHNOLOGIES: Audit technologies are the methods used by various government organizations to monitor the activities of community-based organizations. These technologies are designed to ensure that community-based groups are complying with the criteria of a particular policy or program. They include tracking expenditures and measures of the impact of the programs.

CAPITAL ACCUMULATION: Capital accumulation refers to the addition to the existing wealth of a society through investment of wealth in capital goods. The premise is that such investment leads to increased wealth in a nation and that this benefits the society at large. Capital accumulation and the related growth it brings is distributed unevenly across society. The lack of such growth typically leads to economic stagnation, high unemployment, and the collapse of the economic system.

BEST PRACTICES: Best practices are programs, approaches, or techniques that are held up as having been proven to accomplish a given task effectively. They are used to set standards of treatment or care. The state seeks to develop and disseminate these practices since they provide some assurance of quality without the requirement of legislation. A critical question is whether such practices can be easily moved from context to context given that conditions on the ground have a significant impact on program success.

COMMUNITIES OF INTEREST: A community of interest is a group of people who come together around a shared concern or interest. They typically cross geographic boundaries and may also extend across class, race, and cultural lines.

COMMUNITY: Commonly, the people living in a specific (geographical) location. With the development of transportation and communication technologies, the geographic definition of community has become less dominant as new forms of community have emerged, including communities of interest comprised of like-minded people who may or may not live close to each other and virtual communities that are formed by people who meet and interact online in cyberspace.

COMMUNITY CAPACITY: The ability of a community to meet local needs and to act in the interest of its members. Important aspects of community capacity include sufficient engagement by the members of the community and the resources necessary for them to act. If the state is to successfully download responsibility onto communities, it is essential to build capacity. It cannot build capacity from the outside but can play a supporting role.

CORE FUNDING: State-provided, stable, long-term sources of funds for those providing programs and services in the community, allowing them to plan and provide programs and services on an ongoing basis.

DEREGULATION: The removal of regulations and restrictions, especially those that are related to the functioning of the market economy.

DOWNLOADING: The transfer of the responsibility from higher to lower levels of government to the community and other institutions for the provision of services previously provided by the state, including those it offered in institutional settings (mental health services, services for the developmentally delayed, etc.).

EVALUATION: Evaluation involves the systematic collection of information about a particular program, project, or policy with the aim of providing an assessment of outcomes and effectiveness to various stakeholders (including the state and local organizations).

FACE OF THE COMMUNITY: The face of the community refers to the groups, organizations, and people identified (usually by the state) as legitimately representing the interests and concerns of a community. This may be a community of interest or a geographic community.

GEMEINSCHAFT: Is characterized by informal social relationships and the shared values that connect people and hold groups together.

GESELLSCHAFT: Refers to social relations that are less intimate and more impersonal, based on formal rules and regulations governing appropriate behaviour.

GLOBALIZATION: Globalization is the term developed to name the process of increased interconnectivity of people, groups, organizations, and economies around the globe. Originally the term focused on the increasing interconnection of the world's market and businesses but has been expanded to include the impact on people, groups, and organizations.

GREAT DEPRESSION: Beginning with the collapse of the stock market in 1929, a decade of worldwide poverty and massive unemployment due to the collapse of the economy and the consequences of a serious drought that severely curtailed agricultural production in many parts of North America. The hardships caused by these events were heightened for many individuals and families because of the absence of a social safety net. The Great Depression led to social unrest and conflict.

HOLLOWING OUT (OF THE COMMUNITY): This occurs when community needs and interests are represented by groups and organizations with specialized mandates set by state priorities and when the participation of people living in the community is minimal or nonexistent.

HUMAN CAPITAL: The productive and technical skills that a person has. These skills are garnered through experience and specialized training, and the acquired knowledge contributes to making programs or productive activities that are more effective.

KEYNESIAN WELFARE STATE: A term attributed to societies in which the state provided social supports to its citizens in an effort to reduce the risks associated with the play of market forces. While attributed to John Maynard Keynes's economic theory on state intervention in the markets in response to crises (such as economic depressions), the welfare state actually goes well beyond his proposals to include reducing social inequality and providing support (cash payments and social entitlements) to citizens. These typically include programs that meet basic human needs including health care, universal education, housing, old age security, and assistance if they become unemployed or get hurt on the job.

LAISSEZ-FAIRE: An approach to economic activity that argues that the market is self-correcting and that the state should not intervene in the economy.

LINKAGES: This refers to the connections between and among groups and organizations. There are two types of linkages that are important in community-based work: 1) **HORIZONTAL LINKAGES** are connections between groups and organizations at the same level in the political hierarchy (e.g., between community-based agencies); and 2) **VERTICAL LINKAGES** are connections between community-based organizations and agencies responsible for funding and other core regulatory issues (these are typically government organizations at a political level above that of the community).

MECHANICAL SOLIDARITY: The linking of people based on shared belief and values; these shared beliefs and values provide a basis for collective understanding and work to hold people together.

NEOLIBERALISM: Both a philosophy and political approach to governing that includes the belief that the state's role is to protect individual and property rights. According to this view, the state should not interfere in areas beyond these two and especially should not interfere in the operation of free markets.

NEW PUBLIC MANAGEMENT: This is a government strategy that allows the state to manage an increasingly decentralized provision of programs and services through a variety of techniques including funding criteria, audits, and evaluation. This is a key mechanism through which the state exerts its control over activity at the community level.

ON THE GROUND: Refers to consideration of the events where they are experienced or actually happen.

ORGANIC SOLIDARITY: Social integration based on interrelated needs. Society relies not on shared beliefs and values but on the regulation of relationships among interdependent groups.

PARTNERSHIPS: Occur when groups and organizations work together in a community to address a common concern. See Box 4.1, p. 71.

PRIVATIZATION: The transfer by various government agencies of responsibility for what had been publicly provided services to the private sector (typically for-profit businesses). In Canada, for example, the state-owned energy corporation known as Petro-Canada was sold by the federal government to a private business.

PROJECT FUNDING: The funding of a series of time-limited projects by the state in order to meet its responsibilities. Rather than providing stable and sustainable funding to meet its obligations, including those related to the social safety net, the neoliberal state has replaced this universal approach by short-term targeted funding in areas that match its policy priorities.

PROJECT JUNKIES: An informal term used to describe the impact of the neoliberal funding regime on agencies delivering social support programs. Project junkies have an unhealthy, but necessary, addiction to pursue a seemingly endless series of short-term projects in order to keep their doors open, retain their staff, and serve their clients.

RESPONSIBILIZATION: The process of getting people to accept more responsibility for themselves and their fellow citizens. This process is held out in neoliberal rhetoric as a way of providing benefits to both individuals and to the wider society.

ROLL-BACK NEOLIBERALISM: The dismantling of the Keynesian welfare state's institutions and practices. The term is meant to describe the removal of supports and services previously provided by the state.

ROLL-OUT NEOLIBERALISM: Follows the roll-back phase by introducing alternate means of meeting social needs, including making local groups and agencies (communities) responsible for providing services to those in need.

"SACRED" SOCIAL PROGRAMS: Social programs provide assistance to citizens to meet their needs for support and security. Most countries offer an array of such programs, including universal education and, in some countries, universal health care. Some programs are deemed by citizens to be particularly important, and there is strong resistance to changing or removing them. Such programs are regarded as "scared," that is, of such importance that they are essential and should not be tampered with. In the Canadian context this has included universal health care, pensions, and education.

SILOED: Refers to the separation of groups from one another both within a single organization and within a wider space, such as a community. Siloing delegates responsibility for often overlapping areas to particular individuals and groups without consideration of the interconnections. It results in a lack of information exchange and communication that can lead to the duplication of services or people working at cross-purposes.

THE SOCIAL: The realm of activity in a society through which social support programs and services are provided to people. They reflect minimum standards that people in any particular country associate with being a citizen of that country.

SOCIAL SAFETY NET: The package of social programs provided by the state to support its citizens. In Canada, this includes universal access to health care and education and such things as welfare, old age pensions, and worker's compensation. It is important to realize that these support programs were not always provided by the state. In fact, most were fought for by generations of Canadians who felt that citizens of a wealthy country such as this should be able to share in its prosperity.

SOFT MONEY: One-time funding provided for a project or special purpose. Groups and organizations cannot count on such funding to ensure their ongoing viability. Soft money is project specific and must be applied for on a project-by-project basis.

STEERING AND ROWING: Steering refers to directing the activities of individuals, groups, or organizations, usually at a distance. Those steering set the program agenda. In contrast to steering, rowing is the concept which implies that the individuals, groups, and organizations involved do the actual work required to achieve a particular policy or program outcome. Those doing the rowing do not set the program agenda.

STRUCTURAL DIFFERENTIATION: Involves the increasing specialization of systems and institutions within the society. It is the result of a number of factors including immigration and population growth as well as increased population density and technological change.

TURF: A slang term used to denote the area or range of authority of a person or organization. The term is used to assert ownership of a problem, issue, or area of concern.

References

Atkinson, A.B., and J. Micklewright. 1991. Unemployment compensation and labor market transitions: A critical review. *The Journal of Economic Literature* 29: 1679–27.

Baines, D. 2006. Quantitative indicators "Whose needs are being served?" Quantitative metrics and the reshaping of social services. *Studies in Political Economy* 77 (Spring): 195–209.

Bashevkin, S. 2002. *Welfare hot buttons: Women, work and social policy reform.* Toronto: University of Toronto Press.

Basu, R. 2007. Negotiating acts of citizenship in an era of neoliberal reform: The game of school closures. *International Journal of Urban and Regional Research* 31(1): 109–27.

Bauman, Z. 2001. *Community: Seeking security in an insecure world.* Cambridge: Polity, Blackwell.

Bellefeuille, G., and D. Hemingway. 2005. The new politics of community-based governance requires a fundamental shift in the nature and character of the administrative bureaucracy. *Children and Youth Services Review* 27(5): 491–98.

Bercuson, D. 1990. *Confrontation at Winnipeg: Labour, industrial relations, and the general strike.* Montreal: McGill-Queen's University Press.

Beres, M.A., B. Crow, and L. Gotell. 2009. The perils of institutionalization in neoliberal times: Results of a national survey of Canadian sexual assault and rape crisis centres. *Canadian Journal of Sociology* 34(1): 135–63.

Brenner, N., and N. Theodore. 2002. Cities and the geographies of actually existing neoliberalism. In *Spaces of neoliberalism: Urban restructuring in North America and Western Europe*, ed. N. Brenner and N. Theodore, 2–32. Oxford: Blackwell.

Brooks, C., and S. Cheng. 2001. Declining government confidence and policy preferences in the US: Devolution, regime effects, or symbolic change? *Social Forces* 79(4): 1343–75.

Bruhn, G.G. 2004. *Sociology of Community Connections.* Boston: Springer.

Canada. 2002. *Partnership study: National strategy on community safety and crime prevention.* Phase II summary report. Ottawa, Department of Justice, Evaluation Division (November).

Cameron, S. *The Pickton file.* 2007. Toronto: Knopf Publishers.

Canadian Council on Social Development. 2003. *Funding matters: The impact of Canada's new funding regime on nonprofit and voluntary organizations.* http://www.ccsd.ca/pubs/2003/fm/.

Canadian Factbook on Poverty. 2000. http://www.ccsd.ca/pubs/2000/fbpov00/10-concl.htm.

Caputo, T., K. Kelly, and W. Jamieson. 2001. *The sustainability of social development activities: Some implications for crime prevention.* Ottawa: National Crime Prevention Centre.

Caputo, T., R. Weiler, and J. Anderson. 1997. *The streetlifestyle study.* Health Canada, Office of Alcohol, Drugs and Dependency Issues. Ottawa: Minister of Public Works and Government Services Canada.

Carroll, W.K., and M. Shaw. 2001. Consolidating a neoliberal policy bloc in Canada, 1976 to 1996. *Canadian Public Policy* 27(2): 195–217.

Carson, W.G. 2004. Is communalism dead? Reflections on the present and future practice of crime prevention: Part two. *The Australian and New Zealand Journal of Criminology* 37(2): 192–210.

CBC News In Depth. 2007. The Mulroney years. http://www.cbc.ca/news/background/cdngovernment/mulroney.html.

Cheshire, L., and G. Lawrence. 2005. Neoliberalism, individualization, and community: Regional restructuring in Australia. *Social Identities* 11(5): 435–45.

Clark, J. 1979. Speech. In *The Empire Club of Canada speeches 1978–1979*, ed. R.W. Lewis, 316–27. Toronto: The Empire Club Foundation.

Cohen, S. 1985. *Visions of social control.* Oxford: Polity.

Corcoran, M., S.K. Danziger, and A. Kalil. 2000. How welfare reform is affecting women's work. *Annual Review of Sociology* 26: 241–69.

Crawford, A. 1998. *Crime prevention and community safety: Politics, policies and practices.* Longman Criminology Series. London: Addison Wesley Longman.

Crawford, A. 1999. Questioning appeals to community within crime prevention and control. *European Journal on Criminal Policy and Research* 7(4): 509–30.

Creed, G.W. 2006. Reconsidering community. In *The seductions of community: Emancipations, oppressions, quandaries*, ed. G.W. Creed, 1–24. School of American Research. http://www.sarpress. sarweb.org.

Curry, B., and B. Fenlon. 2008. Conservatives' pro-industry approach compromises food safety, Dion says. *The Globe and Mail* (25 August).

Davidson-Harden, A., L. Kuehn, D. Schugurensky, and H. Smaller. 2009. Neoliberalism and education in Canada. In *The rich world and the impoverishment of education: Diminishing democracy, equity, and workers' rights*, ed. D. Hill, 51–73. New York: Routledge.

Day, G. 2006. *Community and everyday life.* London: Routledge.

Dean, M. 1999. *Governmentality: Power and rule in modern society.* London: Sage.

Defilippis, J., R. Fisher, and E. Shragge. 2006. Neither romance nor regulation: Re-evaluating community. *International Journal of Urban and Regional Research* 30(3): 673–89.

Durkheim, E. 1964. *The division of labour in society.* Glencoe, MN: Free Press. (Orig. pub. 1893.)

Ennis, G., and D. West. 2010. Exploring the potential of social network analysis in asset-based community development practice and research. *Australian Social Work* (1 December). http://www. tandf.co.uk/journals/titles/0312407X.asp.

Etzioni, A. 2000. Utopian visions: Engaged sociologies for the 21st century. *Contemporary Sociology* 29: 188–295.

Fettes, M. 1998. Indigenous education and the ecology of community. *Language, Culture and Curriculum* 11(3): 250–71.

Fontan, J.-M., P. Hamel, R. Morin, and E. Shragge. 2009. Community organizations and local governance in a metropolitan region. *Urban Affairs Review* 44(6): 832–57.

Garland, D. 2001. *The culture of control: Crime and social order in contemporary society.* Chicago: University of Chicago Press.

Gazso, A., and S.A. McDaniel. 2010. The risks of being a lone mother on income support in Canada and the USA. *International Journal of Sociology and Social Policy* 30(7/8): 368–86.

Geddes, M. 2006. Partnership and the limits to local governance in England: Institutionalist analysis and neoliberalism. *International Journal of Urban and Regional Research* 30(1): 76–97.

George, U. 2008. Social policy for tomorrow: A framework for Canadians. *Social Development Issues* 30(3): 1–12.

Gibson, K., S. O'Donnell, and V. Rideout. 2007. The project-funding regime: Complications for community organizations and their staff. *Canadian Public Administration* 50(3): 411–36.

Gough, J. 2002. Neoliberalism and socialization in the contemporary city: Opposites, complements, and instabilities. In *Spaces of neoliberalism: Urban restructuring in North America and Western Europe*, ed. N. Brenner and N. Theodore, 58–79. Oxford: Blackwell.

Graddy, E.A., and D.L. Morgan. 2006. Community foundations, organizational strategy, and public policy. *Nonprofit and Voluntary Sector Quarterly* 35(4): 605–30.

Gray, G. 2009. The responsibilization strategy of health and safety: Neoliberalism and the reconfiguration of individual responsibility for risk (May 2009). *The British Journal of Criminology* 49(3): 326–42.

Habibov, N.N., and L. Fan. 2008. Comparison of inequality reduction and income security in Canada from a mixed to neoliberal welfare regime: Micro-data simulations and policy implications. *Journal of Comparative Social Welfare* 24(1): 33–47.

Hackworth, J., and A. Moriah. 2006. Neoliberalism, contingency, and urban policy: The case of social housing in Ontario. *International Journal of Urban and Regional Research* 30(3): 510–27.

Harmes, A. 2007. The political economy of open federalism. *Canadian Journal of Political Science* 40(2): 417–37.

Hartman, Y. 2005. In bed with the enemy: Some ideas on the connections between neoliberalism and the welfare state. *Current Sociology* 53(1): 57–73.

Harvey, D. 1989. From managerialism to entrepreneurialism: The transformation in urban governance in late capitalism. *Geografiska Annaler B* 71(1): 3–17.

Harvey, D. 2005. *A brief history of neoliberalism.* Oxford: Oxford University Press.

Jackiewicz, E.L. 2006. Community-centered globalization: Modernization under control in rural Costa Rica. *Latin American Perspectives* 33: 136–46.

Keil, R. 2002. "Common-sense" neoliberalism: Progressive conservative urbanism in Toronto, Canada. *Antipode* 34(3): 578–601.

Kolko, G. 1963. *The triumph of conservatism: A re-interpretation of American history, 1900–1916.* New York: Free Press of Glencoe.

Kretzmann, J.P., and J.L. McKnight. 1993. *Building communities from the inside out: A path toward finding and mobilizing a community's assets.* Evanston, IL: Institute for Policy Research.

Kumar, C. 2005. Revisiting community in community-based natural resource management. *Community Development Journal* 40(3): 275–85.

Larner, W. 2006. Unmaking Goliath: Community control in the face of global capital. *Progress in Human Geography* 30(4): 545–46.

Leonard, T. 2010. The dark heart of Disney's dream town. (December 9). http://www.dailymail.co.uk/news/article-1337026/Celebration-murder-suicide-wife-swapping-Disneys-dark-dream-town.html.

Levi, R. 2008. Auditable community: The moral order of Megan's Law. *British Journal of Criminology* 48(5): 583–603.

Levitan-Reid, E. 2006. *Towards an asset-based, resident-led neighbourhood development strategy: Reflections on action for neighbourhood change (February 2005–March 2006).* Ottawa: Caledon Institute of Social Policy (7 June).

Maclennan, D. 2006. *Remaking neighbourhood renewal: Towards creative neighbourhood renewal policies for Britain.* Ottawa: Caledon Institute of Social Policy (February).

Mahon, R. 2005. Rescaling social reproduction: Childcare in Toronto/Canada and Stockholm/Sweden. *International Journal of Urban and Regional Research* 29(2): 341–57.

McCold, P., and T. Wachtel. 2003. In pursuit of a paradigm: A theory of restorative justice. International Institute for Restorative Practices (Real Justice) website, http://www.realjustice.org/uploads/ article_pdfs/paradigm.pdf.

McGrath, S., U. George, B. Lell, and K. Moffat. 2007. Seeking social justice: Community practice within diverse marginalized populations in Canada. *Social Development Issues* 29(2): 77–91.

McKnight, J.L., and J.P. Kretzmann. 1996. *Mapping community capacity.* Evanston, IL: The Asset-Based Community Development Institute, Institute for Policy Research, Northwestern University.

Meagher, S. N.d. *A neighbourhood vitality index: An approach to measuring neighbourhood well-being.* Toronto: United Way of Greater Toronto.

Miller, B. 2007. Modes of governance, modes of resistance: Contesting neoliberalism in Calgary. In *Contesting Neoliberalism*, ed. H. Leitner, J. Pect, and E.S. Sheppard, 223–49. New York: Guilford Press.

Mitchell, K. 2001. Transnationalism, neoliberalism, and the rise of the shadow state. *Economy and Society* 30: 165–89.

Mitchell, K. 2004. *Crossing the neoliberal line: Pacific Rim migration and the metropolis.* Philadelphia: Temple University Press.

NPR. 2008. A Depression-era anthem for our times. (15 November). http://www.npr.org/templates/story/story.php?storyId=96654742.

O'Connor, J.R. 1973. *The fiscal crisis of the state.* New York: Macmillan.

Olsen, G.M. 2002. *The politics of the welfare state: Canada, Sweden, and the United States.* Toronto: Oxford University Press.

O'Malley, P. 1992. Risk, power and crime prevention. *Economy and Society* 21: 252–75.

Orsini, M. 2006. From "community run" to "community based"? Exploring the dynamics of civil society-state transformation in urban Montreal. *Canadian Journal of Urban Research* 15(1): 22–40.

Pavey, J.L., A.B. Muth, D. Ostermeier, and M. Davis. 2007. Building capacity for local governance: An application of interactional theory to developing a community of interest. *Rural Sociology* 72(1): 90–110.

Pavlich, G. 1996. The power of community mediation: Government and formation of self identity. *Law and Society Review* 30(4): 707–33.

Peck, J., and A. Tickell. 2002. Neoliberalizing space. In *Spaces of neoliberalism: Urban restructuring in North America and Western Europe*, ed. N. Brenner and N. Theodore, 33–57. Oxford: Blackwell.

Phillips, S., and K. Lavasseur. 2004. The snakes and ladders of accountability: Contradictions between contracting and collaboration for Canada's voluntary sector. *Canadian Public Administration* 47(4): 451–74.

Putnam, R. 1995. Bowling alone. *Journal of Democracy* 6(1): 65–78.

Putnam, R. 2000. *Bowling alone: The collapse and revival of the American community.* New York: Simon and Schuster.

Read, A. 2009. Psychiatric deinstitutionalization in BC: Negative consequences and possible solutions. *University of British Columbia Medical Journal* 1(1): 25–26.

Richmond, T., and J. Shields. 2004. NGO restructuring: Constraints and consequences. *Canadian Review of Social Policy* (Spring/Summer): 53–67.

Rist, C., and L. Humphrey. 2010. City and community innovations in CDAs: The role of community-based organizations. *Children and Youth Services Review* 32(11): 1520–27.

Rochefort, D.A., M. Rosenberg, and D. White. 1998. Community as a policy instrument: A comparative analysis. *Policy Studies Journal* 26(3): 548–68.

Rose, N. 1996. The death of the social? Re-figuring the territory of government. *Economy and Society* 25(3): 327–56.

Rose, N. 1999. The third way: The renewal of social democracy. *Economy and Society* 28(3): 467–93.

Rose, L.E., and P.A. Pettersen. 2000. The legitimacy of local government: What makes a difference? Evidence from Norway. *Research in Urban Policy* 8: 25–65.

Sandler, J. 2007. Community-based practices: Integrating dissemination theory with critical theories of power and justice. *American Journal of Community Psychology* 40(3/4): 272–89.

Schofield, B. 2002. Partners in power: Governing the Self-Sustaining Community. *Sociology* 36(3): 663–83.

Search Institute. 2002. *Assets Checklist.* http://www.search-institute.org/.

Silver, S., J. Shields, S. Wilson, and A. Scholtz. 2005. The excluded, the vulnerable and the reintegrated in a neoliberal era: Qualitative dimensions of the unemployment experience. *Socialist Studies* 1(1): 31–56.

Snider, L. 2004. Resisting neo-liberalism: The poisoned water disaster in Walkerton, Ontario. *Social and Legal Studies* 13(2): 265–89.

Statistics Canada. 2008. The Great Depression. http://www65.statcan.gc.ca/acyb01/acyb01_0005-eng.htm.

Stenson, K., and P. Watt. 1999. Governmentality and "the death of the social"?: A discourse analysis of local government texts in south-east England. *Urban Studies* 36(1): 189–201.

Stohr, M.K., C. Hemmens, B. Shapiro, B. Chambers, and L. Kelley. 2002. Comparing inmate perceptions of two residential substance abuse treatment programs. *International Journal of Offender Therapy and Comparative Criminology* 46(6): 699–714.

Tang, K., and H. Peters. 2006. Internationalizing the struggle against neoliberal social policy: The experience of Canadian women. *International Social Work* 49(5): 571–82.

Thatcher, M. 1987. Interview, *Women's Own*, 31 October 1987. http://www.margaretthatcher.org/document/106689.

Thorsen, D.E., and A. Lie. n.d. *What is Neoliberalism?* http://folk.uio.no/daget/What%20is%20Neo-Liberalism%20FINAL.pdf.

Tönnies, F. 1955. *Community and association.* London: Routledge and Kegan Paul. (Orig. pub. 1887.)

Torjman, S. 2007. *Repairing Canada's social safety net.* Ottawa: The Caledon Institute of Social Policy.

Turner, D., and S. Martin. 2003. Managerialism meets community development: Contracting for social inclusion? *Policy and Politics* 32(1): 21–32.

Turner, J.H., and N.A. Dolch. 1996. Using classical theorists to reconceptualize community dynamics. *Research in Community Sociology* 6: 19–36.

United Way–Action for Neighbourhood Change. 2007. *Rebuilding neighbourhoods: A neighbourhood vitality index (draft).* Ottawa: United Way of Canada (March).

Valverde, M. 1991. *The age of light, soap, and water: Moral reform in English Canada 1885–1925.* Toronto: McClelland and Stewart.

Voas, D., and A. Crockett. 2005. Religion in Britain: Neither believing nor belonging. *Sociology* 39(1): 11–28.

Whiteside, H. 2009. Canada's health care "crisis": Accumulation by dispossession and the neoliberal fix. *Studies in Political Economy* (84): 79–100.

Index